The MORE MINDSET

DIANA PAGANO

Foreword by Marie Diamond, from *The Secret*

The MORE MINDSET

**BREAK MENTAL LIMITS
AND STEP INTO
EXTRAORDINARY RESULTS**

WILEY

Copyright © 2026 by DP International, LLC. All rights reserved.

Published by John Wiley & Sons, Inc., Hoboken, New Jersey.

No part of this publication may be reproduced, stored in a retrieval system, or transmitted in any form or by any means, electronic, mechanical, photocopying, recording, scanning, or otherwise, except as permitted under Section 107 or 108 of the 1976 United States Copyright Act, without either the prior written permission of the Publisher, or authorization through payment of the appropriate per-copy fee to the Copyright Clearance Center, Inc., 222 Rosewood Drive, Danvers, MA 01923, (978) 750-8400, fax (978) 750-4470, or on the web at www.copyright.com. Requests to the Publisher for permission should be addressed to the Permissions Department, John Wiley & Sons, Inc., 111 River Street, Hoboken, NJ 07030, (201) 748-6011, fax (201) 748-6008, or online at http://www.wiley.com/go/permission.

The manufacturer's authorized representative according to the EU General Product Safety Regulation is Wiley-VCH GmbH, Boschstr. 12, 69469 Weinheim, Germany, e-mail: Product_Safety@wiley.com.

Trademarks: Wiley and the Wiley logo are trademarks or registered trademarks of John Wiley & Sons, Inc. and/or its affiliates in the United States and other countries and may not be used without written permission. All other trademarks are the property of their respective owners. John Wiley & Sons, Inc. is not associated with any product or vendor mentioned in this book.

Limit of Liability/Disclaimer of Warranty: While the publisher and the author have used their best efforts in preparing this work, including a review of the content of the work, neither the publisher nor the authors make any representations or warranties with respect to the accuracy or completeness of the contents of this work and specifically disclaim all warranties, including without limitation any implied warranties of merchantability or fitness for a particular purpose. No warranty may be created or extended by sales representatives, written sales materials, or promotional statements for this work. The fact that an organization, website, or product is referred to in this work as a citation and/or potential source of further information does not mean that the publisher and author endorse the information or services the organization, website, or product may provide or recommendations it may make. This work is sold with the understanding that the publisher is not engaged in rendering professional services. The advice and strategies contained herein may not be suitable for your situation. You should consult with a specialist where appropriate. Further, readers should be aware that websites listed in this work may have changed or disappeared between when this work was written and when it is read. Neither the publisher nor author shall be liable for any loss of profit or any other commercial damages, including but not limited to special, incidental, consequential, or other damages.

For general information on our other products and services or for technical support, please contact our Customer Care Department within the United States at (800) 762-2974, outside the United States at (317) 572-3993 or fax (317) 572-4002.

Wiley also publishes its books in a variety of electronic formats. Some content that appears in print may not be available in electronic formats. For more information about Wiley products, visit our website at www.wiley.com.

Library of Congress Cataloging-in-Publication Data is Available:

ISBN 9781394388684 (Cloth)
ISBN 9781394388691 (ePub)
ISBN 9781394388707 (ePDF)

Cover Design: Jon Boylan
Cover Image: © Bokehstore/stock.adobe.com
Author Photo: DP International, LLC
SKY10132066_112025

*To my mom,
who taught me faith,
and that with God
all things are possible.
Thank you for believing in me
when at times, I struggled to.
You are my rock.*

Contents

Foreword by Marie Diamond   ix

Introduction   xi

Chapter 1   You Are What You Believe   1

Chapter 2   The Power to Make a New Choice   21

Chapter 3   Breathing During the Storm   43

Chapter 4   Happiness Is Not Something You Seek   65

Chapter 5   Sorry, Not Sorry   89

Chapter 6   Change the Channel   111

Chapter 7   A Time to Move, a Time to Be Still   131

Chapter 8   God's Daily Dosage   149

Chapter 9   Visualization on Steroids   169

Chapter 10   Barriers Overrated   185

Chapter 11	Create a Life Worth Living	199
Chapter 12	Be Open to Receive . . . More	213
Acknowledgments		*229*
About the Author		*231*
Index		*233*

Foreword by Marie Diamond

From the very first moment I met Diana Pagano, I felt her vibrant, magnetic energy. She is a rare force—determined, authentic, and deeply committed to helping others step into their highest potential. In a world where so many people settle for "just enough," Diana stands as a reminder that life is meant to be lived fully, boldly, and with purpose.

In *The More Mindset*, Diana doesn't simply share her story—she offers a powerful road map for transformation. With honesty and courage, she guides you through a journey of shifting from fear to confidence, from hesitation to bold action, and from scarcity to abundance. Her insights, strategies, and practical exercises are infused with both heart and wisdom, inviting you not only to be inspired but to take action and implement real change.

What makes this book extraordinary is Diana's gift for blending inspiration with practicality. She shows us that mindset is not just about positive thinking—it is about aligning your thoughts, energy, and actions so that you create meaningful results. Each page calls you to embrace possibility, claim your power, and step courageously into the life you were always meant to live.

If you are ready for more—more confidence, more clarity, more joy, and more success—this book will empower you to take the driver's seat of your destiny. Diana Pagano is living proof that mindset is everything, and through *The More Mindset*, she lights the path for each of us to realize that we, too, are capable of far more than we ever imagined.

With love and light,
Marie Diamond
Master Teacher in The Secret and Global Bestselling Author

Introduction

Dear Reader,

When life can be hectic and moving so fast, with a constant stream of digital information at our fingertips 24/7, it makes me extremely happy to know that you are holding this physical book in your hands.

These words are my gift to YOU.

You, the person who wants something more, whatever more means to you. You may even feel stuck. You, the one with the fire in your heart and who refuses to settle. You, the person who has the courage to dream big and is willing to fight for it—this is your reminder: you're not crazy. You're courageous.

This isn't a book for a "quick fix." It's a flashlight in a dark room. It's a map for your future. It's a mirror of your life. You might not like what you see, initially. But knowing where to start, knowing what you need to change, and how to change it, will help you get to a place where everything is possible.

You'll see yourself more clearly. Change the thoughts that hold you back and find your way forward—to that destination that lights your heart on fire!

At different times in my life, I was yearning for more and I wish—*I so wish*—I had this book to hold in my hands when I struggled, when I was looking for a road map to the life of *my* dreams.

The life you have always dreamed of awaits you on the other side of this book!

Today, holding this book, you are standing at the edge of a transformational shift—one that will uncover a powerful gift God placed within you: the ability to see and live life to the fullest.

That doesn't mean you will have a life without challenges; but I promise you this—once you understand the teachings in *The More Mindset*, you'll see them through an entirely different lens.

The path to the life you've been longing for—peace, purpose, and success—will become not just visible, but attainable. This is where real, lasting change begins—with clarity and intention!

And if you're shaking your head and wondering how you can make this shift?

I get it because I questioned this, too. Looking for that missing piece to the puzzle. Raised where the odds were stacked against me, I survived and thrived.

Yet, having reached the pinnacle of success, residual feelings still held me back, restraining me in key areas of my life, manifesting as a sense of feeling lost, not being enough, caught up in the hustle, moving fast through life, always chasing that dream, yet never arriving. Although successful on the outside, sort of, I was not living with real purpose nor true fulfillment.

I was searching for answers, too. Like you, I picked up a book at the bookstore, curious about what I might find inside, I read it and wondered: could this be the one, the one with the road map?

I've read so many amazing books, each one offering hope, strategies, and the promise of transformation. Even though each had its unique focus on how to change my beliefs to reach the other side, they lacked something; that key ingredient I was searching for. They didn't have what I thought I needed, but at the time could not pinpoint what it was. Deep down, I knew there had to be a better way; I just didn't know where to begin.

It took me years to acquire the understanding that I now have. In this book, I cover it all. What I discovered on my journey was both humbling and empowering: the power to change had always been in my own hands. God gave each and every one of us the tools to create the life we're meant for. But having the tools doesn't equal success. No, not really. Not when you feel every day that you are losing yourself in life's whirlwind of noise and chaos. It is hard to pull yourself out and look in the mirror—to see the *truth*.

As a little girl, I worried constantly. Would today be the day my mother had another nervous breakdown? Would I have to, again, rub alcohol on her arms to bring her back?

I lived in fear of eviction, wondering where we'd sleep next. We moved every other year from the time I was born until I was 17. With every move I wondered if this could finally be the house that felt like home, or would we have to move again, leaving behind the friends I had just started to make?

This instability followed me into young adulthood. I tried to take care of my parents emotionally, and sometimes even financially. I remember one of my first big paychecks at age 16. I had dreams of going to Disneyland; but instead, I handed that $275 check over to my parents to keep our electricity from being shut off.

I wasn't mad. Sure, yes, I was a little sad. But I felt a sense of responsibility to help.

My dream was put on hold. And throughout my life this has been a pattern.

"You will marry our daughter since she was a virgin when you met her," my Catholic parents told my boyfriend. I married young—instead of a senior prom, I had a wedding. I was pregnant and, deep down, relieved. Maybe this was my escape. But my life—my prospects, my dreams—everything was on hold, yet again. Nevertheless, although scared, I was happy I was going to be a young mom.

As a single mom living in Scottsdale and a rookie entrepreneur, managing my real estate career, people thought I had it all together. But inside, I was searching and longing for something more. And guess what? The moment I raised my standards of what my life was to the life I dreamed of, everything changed. I started asking the right questions.

And the right questions will do this for you, too—that I promise you.

The answers that had been there all along began to show up for me. Things started to change in my life. The home I promised I'd give my kids. Security. My dream car I once said I would have—I had that, too. Financial stability showed up in my bank account. I traveled the world, which was one of my dreams (my first flight ever was not until I was 24). I met my now husband because I was ready and open to receive. And I always knew that I would have two boys a year or two apart in my thirties. Exactly and precisely as I imagined it, is how it happened. At first, I thought, could this be real? Is this a coincidence? Or are the tools I'm utilizing to change my thoughts, behaviors, and expectations of myself and my environment really playing a role?

I continued using all that I learned and through my experience and with that came even more evidence that I was in fact creating the life I imagined. It became my reality because of the mindset shifts I cultivated. These shifts helped me grow a multimillion-dollar foreign language company to 5× its size as the EVP, when others saw it as impossible. And if it were not for the tools I share in this book, none of it would have been possible.

Introduction

I have had the honor to witness bold transformations during my coaching career. These tools I share as a motivational speaker and published author ignite a spark of hope to what's possible.

This book is a testament to show that inspiration can emerge from life's challenges. Your pain is your power. When I began writing, I cried through out these chapter. It was therapeutic. Finally, I was releasing the pain through my words. I've always pushed forward, always kept things moving. But in writing this, it allowed me to slow down and realize that although my pain almost broke me it confirmed there was a bigger purpose awaiting me on the other side. My life path, although hard, was not in vain; it was preparing me because of my calling being so much bigger than this. I felt God's message, so clear. To help others change their life. Because life does not have to be hard.

Our upbringing, what we've been exposed to and endured, has conditioned us into believing we must complicate life, when there's no need to.

This book is my way of helping you see the path in front of you more clearly—and walk it with confidence. Whatever your story is, no matter the shoes you've walked in, there's one thing you always have control over: what you choose to put up with. This includes behaviors that you maintain. You are the one who will break the cycle—I promise you that. You'll do it the moment you're too tired to stay stuck, when you're ready for something better. You can do it! I know you can!

As a little girl, I would dream of a beautiful, "normal life"—a life that didn't just exist in a fantasy book. And eventually I learned that dream wasn't fantasy.

It was within reach!

You *can* become the person you dream of being.

This book is for all of you searching for that missing piece—that one thing that makes everything finally click.

After years of speaking to audiences and hearing stories just like mine and yours, and answering questions just like the ones stuck in my head, and the ones plaguing you, I felt a deep pull to put everything I've learned into a practical format that people far and wide had access to, those ready for change.

"Change the channel" is a *tool* I teach in this book that will change your life. It is about recognizing when the current script isn't working and shifting your perspective, behavior, or approach. How the way we think shapes the way we live. Our beliefs and thoughts act as "internal channels" that constantly play in the background of our mind. It's not about ignoring challenges—it's about reframing them, rewriting your story, and reclaiming control of your narrative.

When we learn to change those channels with intention, everything around us begins to change, too. And that change shows us that life doesn't have to be hard. Even with its twists, turns, and challenges, life can still be beautiful, exciting, and fulfilling (full of purpose).

And my words, the ones in this book—will guide you and remind you of the power you already have within. That is why my goal is to help you take back control of your inner self, so you can begin to shape your outer one with clarity and intention.

I promise you that what I share with you will be simple and practical, and no matter what your past holds, your future will be brighter and more fulfilling than ever before.

I thought a lot about YOU, the person who needed to read this book the most. Pain, its longing, and the desire for a better life, does not discriminate . . . regardless of your ethnicity. Whether you're rich or poor—we all want to belong. We all want to feel worthy. This book is for those who want real change.

Maybe you think it's too late or that your life can't possibly turn around. But I've been there, and I am going to challenge your thinking. My hope is that you will reach a moment where you will have some "aha" moments. Or, say, "*Wow, I never saw things that way,*" or "*Wow, I did not know the science behind our mind,*" and from that point on, you will approach every situation with a completely new mindset.

As someone who triumphed over significant personal and professional hurdles—I bring practical, candid, and straightforward advice to you, the ambitious reader, the one who doesn't want to settle! In this book, you'll walk with a new kind of faith. My faith in God has always been strong, but it deepened to an entirely new level when I started applying the teachings I'm sharing in *The More Mindset* to my own life. At the core, we all want to feel like our life has meaning.

The More Mindset is about building a life—brick by brick. No shortcuts. But this time, you will be laying the kind of foundation that will weather *any* storm. You won't just think positive thoughts. You'll build something solid, something real.

Of course, I can't promise you that you won't experience challenges. But I *can* promise you this: you'll never face them the same way again.

What will you get out of this book? You will gain a robust understanding of how to harness the power of your thoughts to change your life's trajectory, develop deeper self-awareness, and learn transformative habits that foster personal growth and fulfillment.

Whether you're trying to find direction in a world overrun by technology that rewards instant gratification, or you're a leader carrying the weight of others' expectations, or an entrepreneur who's achieved success but still feels unfulfilled, or maybe you're just ready to get to that next level, this book is for you. It's for the working or stay-at-home mom juggling everything while quietly feeling lost, and for the caregivers who've poured themselves into others for so long they've forgotten who they are. If you're recovering from loss or burnout, or if you simply feel deep down that life is meant to be more than just surviving—I wrote this book as a guide for you, to meet you where you are, and become the best you that you can be, to live more boldly, and go for what you want! And never settle. Because you are capable to go as big as you feel like going.

I believe you are here for a greater purpose than you have even realized. If you're ready to feel empowered and inspired, to break through limits and step fully into your calling, it's time to *change the channel* and start living the life you were always meant to live. And remember, God created you as a masterpiece—and even with your imperfections—you are already perfect.

Stay Blessed and go *Make Things Happen!*

Diana Pagano

CHAPTER 1

You Are What You Believe

I hung up the phone and my heart sank. I called my nanny in a rush, trying to get dressed and putting on make-up while instructing my eldest to finish his homework and make sure his sister finished her dinner.

I could feel adrenaline coursing through my veins. I was a mixed ball of emotions: enthusiasm, desperation, and guilt. I tried my best to contain my enthusiasm and desperation for the sale. I needed this real estate deal, because this was the one that would keep our mortgage paid, and prevent my family from living the same cycle I did as a child, having to move often due to financial struggles my parents faced. Then there was that persistent guilt that kept gnawing at me; the kind I couldn't suppress… nor ignore. It was the guilt of having to rush out the door the moment the phone would ring with the opportunity of a sale. I felt the guilt of missing out on quality time. "Was I a bad mom?" I kept asking myself, as these feelings bounced about within. There had to be a better way of living than this.

My fake eyelash unglued. That's all it took. I collapsed on the couch. And I lost it. In some ways a part of me used this unexpected eyelash drama to cry, just cry. To cry in silence. My tears were *not* from the exhaustion of having to work seven days a week. My tears came from the exhaustion of having to always to be "on"—mentally; my tears came from the stress and complexities of single-parent juggling… while simultaneously presenting to the world a facade of being myself. I didn't need just a break; I needed a better way than living life this way. I always felt that there was a better way; I just didn't know how or what it was, at the time.

In my career as a real estate agent, I pushed myself to the limit. Why? To provide for my children. To give them more than what I had growing up; that moment and day, which I remember clearly… when I chose to end my abusive marriage. I made a promise to myself, and to my children, that they would never experience the anguish, the struggles, and the constant fear as I did. They would never experience the uncertainties of a residential nomad, the constant settling, uprooting, and moving into 13 different homes by the time they turned 18. Never again!

I would do it all. Be their mom, their dad (at times), a friend, a confidante, attend every school event, and celebrate milestones they achieved. This I vowed… all while making sure I provided the comfort and stability my children needed, that my childhood lacked.

And here I was, bawling on my couch over a damn fake eyelash. Pathetic. What was this all about? I made it; I secured the successful single-mother prize in all areas: materially, outwardly, socially. Meals were never a concern. I could afford a nanny, which was a godsend. I made every school event... well, mostly... at the last minute. But I was making it. That was what mattered. Or was it?

Engrossed in the relentless pursuit of success, driven by the allure of a lucrative fat paycheck and the thrill of constant achievement, I became hyper-focused on attaining goals—the goal to move to the best neighborhood; the goal to drive a better car. The goal to travel with my kids and pay for expensive hotels and order room service; the goal to be #1 agent in my office. Basically, a life that I never knew existed as a child.

This relentless drive, however, obscured the essence of "being"—experiencing the present moment and cultivating inner peace, bathing in God's blessings, living. The notion of "stopping to smell the roses" was utterly foreign to me. I didn't stop to recognize all of my hard work and really tell myself, "Diana, be proud of yourself. You're doing fantastic!" I lost this opportunity to embrace presence because of the constant worry or distraction of being "on"—24/7. The constant—what felt like—rat race.

Outwardly I presented an image of enviable "perfection." That was the tip of the iceberg. But inside? I was slipping, floating away, losing myself. Have you ever felt this way? Possessed by this overwhelming feeling where, on the surface, the facade you present to the world is, *"Hey, I got it together."* And secretly... below this iceberg, what no one sees and feels, you are paddling, struggling with all your might, just enough, so you don't sink. That frozen public smile is just an illusion; for it is truly a grimace, rather than an expression of joy. Questioning your path, do you ever ask yourself:

> *"Is there a better way?"*
> *"What is it that I am missing?"*
> *"How do others do it?"*

I did. And it took me years of relentless effort, fueled by the belief that I had to work tirelessly, alone to the bone, and without respite, to succeed. This journey was a grueling gauntlet of trials and errors, of struggles and failures, many of which inflicted immense pain. But it was through navigating this challenging path that I ultimately forged my way toward success.

My story is why I'm compelled to share my experiences, my discoveries, my tears, and my joys. If I can shorten your journey of becoming the best version of yourself, where you live your life devoid of self-imposed limitations, living without regrets, where you tap into your fullest potential, with confidence and a belief in yourself way bigger than anything or anyone could ever break, then I've accomplished my mission in writing this book. Life does not have to be hard. Ironically, I grew up thinking otherwise, that life had to be hard. That was my reality; that was the belief I absorbed as a young kid.

How was that belief installed into my mind from childhood? Great question; one of many that I'll answer throughout. And rest assured… here is the cold, brutal fact of reality: Yes, you may go through hard and challenging moments, but it can still be beautiful, and a life you can feel proud of because you now will know how to navigate through it in a way that is to your greater benefit, where you get to create a life of real purpose and fulfillment.

You Are What You Believe

We all have heard a version of this adage: "Tell me what *(fill in the blank: What you eat? Who are your friends? What books you read? Etc.)*, and I will tell you who you are." This cliché is partially true! You are what you believe you are. I'll say it again in a different way:

"We are what we believe." From the moment you enter this world your beliefs are shaping you. For example:

- *If you don't get As and Bs you're not smart.*
- *Looking at the moon will damage your eyes.*
- *If you touch it, it will burn you.*

Beliefs, acquired both consciously and unconsciously throughout our lives, actively construct who we are, influencing our self-image and confidence. They shape our understanding of the world and guide our chosen perspective, ultimately impacting our expectations, goals, and dreams. Beliefs can be, and often are, passed from one generation to another, without challenging their validity or origin. We absorb these unquestioned beliefs on face value because we trust the source. Oftentimes these "psychological DNA-like residues" belong to our parents, our teachers, our friends, and the social network around us—our village.

Take for example, "You can't eat bananas at night, or you will get an upset stomach" (my grandmother told my mom and she, in turn, passed it down to me). Another example, we now know that eggs are not a part of the dairy group. I realized this later in life well into my 30s. But as a child growing up during the 1980s, the entire school system ill-informed us about eggs and their food group classification. The memory is still sharp in my mind to this day—sitting on the classroom carpet with my classmates in kindergarten, that precise key moment when a certain belief was subtly, yet effectively, "integrated" into our understanding.

Some of these unquestioned, long-held beliefs can serve a valuable purpose. They contribute to our safety, provide a framework for understanding the world, and guide us in becoming admirable individuals, productive members of society, and emotionally competent partners and parents. Some fundamental examples of such beneficial beliefs include: "Return kindness with kindness," "Look both ways before crossing the street," "Treat others as you want to be treated," "Maintain proper hygiene health by washing your hands," and "Brush your teeth, or you'll get bugs in your teeth." *(God knows I have used this more times than I care to admit.)* And so on and so forth.

As with everything in life and the universe there is a dark side. In order to function as healthy human beings, we need to be aware of this universal yin/yang principle, for example, good/bad, night/day, hot/cold, sadness/happiness, failure/success. This binary principle is endless. It's true… though we forget—to our detriment. Nevertheless, we need to be aware that this universal energetic principle is nonjudgmental, does not discriminate, and works hand in hand. For you to appreciate success, you have to experience failure. For us to relish in happiness, we have to experience sadness. Where and what you place your attention on is where your energy and intention flow toward. It not only affects us, but it also influences our environment and loved ones close to and around us.

False Beliefs/Believing the Lies

The saying, "What you don't know won't hurt you," is not only a joke; it is a dangerous fallacy. While ignorance might shield us from some unpleasant truths, it can also be deeply detrimental. There's a wealth of knowledge out there that could be empowering and beneficial; yet it remains inaccessible due to our lack of awareness. This ignorance, however, does not diminish the potential harm it could cause.

Beliefs accumulated contribute to building the individual we are today, as well as our mindset that we use to maneuver through the world. Some beliefs are positive; some are negative, to the point they harm us on the psychological level, while others paralyze our progress toward success, making it impossible to achieve goals, to become our true selves, and from fulfilling the potential that we were all given by God. Not convinced? Think about this: From the moment we are born into this world, social forces such as our parents and family members, our peers, our teachers, TV, and (now) social media bombard us with beliefs. They exert significant control over our lives, dictating our language, our culinary preferences, our friendships, our academic interests, and much more.

A significant portion of our self-image and ego is formed by the age of 10, largely shaped by the messages we receive and accept without question during these formative years. These influences stem from the actions and teachings of others, as well as our own experiences, reading, storytelling, and even traumatic events. These early beliefs continue to exert a profound influence throughout our lives. For example, as a child, my mother frequently warned me that I would catch a cold if I didn't wear socks. I also firmly believed that swimming immediately after eating was forbidden. Some of these beliefs may seem harmless, even a bit eccentric, for example:

"You have to wait two days to call back your date."
"If you swallow gum it stays in your stomach for seven years."

While seemingly harmless, even comical or absurd, some of the beliefs we acquire in childhood can have surprisingly detrimental effects on our development, continuing into adulthood, while others have more significant implications.

- *"You are ugly."*
- *"You have horse teeth like your father."*
- *"You are stupid."*
- *"You're not good at music."*

- *"Girls can't play baseball."*
- *"You would never be able to do this."*
- *"You are so clumsy."*
- *"Life isn't fair."* *

* I cannot stand this one. I can't tell you how many times I hear this and I think it's bullshit. Yes, life can have its challenges, but life is what YOU make of it. IF you believe life isn't fair then your life experiences will constantly support this belief.

Should I go on?

I remember taking my daughter to the pediatrician. During our visit the doctor came in and asked my daughter what she enjoys doing for fun?

"Playing the piano," my daughter replied.

"I was never good at music," the pediatrician casually said, as if it was second nature to say.

Alarm bells immediately rang in my mind.

"How do you know that you're not good at music?" I asked the pediatrician.

"Oh, my music teacher in elementary school *always* told me that," the pediatrician replied.

Talk about limiting and harmful beliefs! Though the music teacher's intentions may not have been malicious, perhaps stemming from a misguided attempt at "tough love," or an ill-conceived effort to inspire greater dedication to practice, her comments inadvertently left a lasting scar on the mind of this now middle-aged woman, a pediatrician. This deeply ingrained belief in her own musical inadequacy, stemming from a childhood experience in elementary school, has had a deep and lasting impact on her life.

As I sat on my couch, sobbing over the ruined fake eyelash, a profound realization struck me: my relentless, unsparing work schedule, to the detriment of myself and my kids, was fueled by the false belief that "Seven-day workweeks were essential for success!" Where, when, and how was this belief implanted? What was the source? My upbringing. That's *"where, when, and how."* Every single day of my childhood—I saw my parents living this belief! It had nothing to do with what I was told as a belief; it was what I *saw*. While my parents did the best they could with what they knew, they still struggled, constantly working! There were no "vacations." Working seven days a week was the norm, and subconsciously I thought *"I HAVE to work seven days a week to survive life... to get anywhere in life."* Life HAD to be a struggle. That was the example I was presented with, and consequently, that behavior became ingrained as the norm in my own understanding of the world.

Adding to this as a single mom with the responsibility of taking care of two kids practically on my own, and having recently ended a psychologically noxious relationship, I pursued real estate, as if my life depended on it; to be frank—it did! I wanted to give my kids something more than what I had growing up. This was my driver. I was going to succeed—or die trying. And yes, YES, with God's blessing, I was successful, and darn proud of it. But I also had my failures and fears, too.

There were days I didn't know how I was going to pay for my mortgage. I was so focused on chasing versus living with intention, and so riveted on irrelevant details that I failed to grasp the larger picture. I wasn't investing my energy into what really mattered; I was doing it all wrong. Compounding this, the sum total of my childhood trauma and fears, learned and experienced, acted as the fuel that I used to push myself toward success. What were some of these fears?

- Insufficient money to pay the rent and thus getting evicted.
- Lack of a stable home as a result of constantly uprooting and moving to a new place to live.
- Survival fears.

I endured a number of painful childhood experiences, and I was determined to ensure my children did not suffer similarly. My greatest challenge, however, lay in overcoming the limiting beliefs that had taken root within me. Through this journey of self-discovery, I have gained a profound understanding of how our mindsets and beliefs shape our reality. Now, I use this knowledge to empower and teach others how to harness the transformative power of this positive mental game.

Your Vibration Will Determine What You Attract (What You Think, You Attract)

I grew up with a friend who is beautiful inside and out. However, like many, she carries limiting beliefs that hinder her personal growth. One such belief is that "all men are jerks." This belief, unfortunately, seems to attract men who confirm her negative expectations, clarifying why such a remarkable and exceptional individual consistently attracts relationships that diminish her self-worth and fail to nurture her potential.

This example is not an exception. There are so many people who are in similar situations, restrained by perception in what they see as reality, not seeing their part and taking responsibility for what holds them back, not questioning the decisions they made or continue to make, and lacking the understanding that to be loved, we must first love ourselves unconditionally. And no, doing your nails, going to the gym, or doing your hair and makeup is not the definition of loving yourself. You love yourself by being kind. By owning your story without shame. Talking to yourself with compassion. Making decisions that serve you. Raising yourself to a different standard. Question your circumstances, whether it is about love, finance, or anything else. Challenge them. This is when the doorway to change opens, welcoming you.

Case in point—I shared with you how I was stuck on the seven-day hamster wheel of survival, and questioning that there had to be more to life. I was hungry to understand the *"whys"* of my circumstance, so I read every book that focused on the power of the subconscious mind and how it affects our brain and our physical body.

I dedicated myself to reading books that challenged my deeply held beliefs, prompting rigorous self-reflection on how these beliefs shaped my thoughts, attitudes, and ultimately my actions. I delved into the realm of quantum physics, exploring its profound impact on everyday life. As I integrated this new knowledge into my life, I witnessed remarkable transformations. Though they did not all happen overnight, it was a beautiful process of self-discovery. Eventually, I reached a point of no return—a profound shift in consciousness. I now live in accordance with my newfound understanding of the subconscious mind and its profound influence on our lives. These discoveries have fundamentally altered the trajectory of my life. For me this was the event horizon.

"There must be others struggling like me for answers," I thought. I felt a strong calling and responsibility to share all that I knew, what I discovered. And at the time of the writing of this book, I continue to unearth more. Nicola Tesla said, "If you want to find the secrets of the universe, think in terms of energy, frequency, and vibration." I think back to that time of my insatiable appetite for knowledge and how fascinating, scary, and wonderful it felt to understand that... I have control over my mindset, control over my subconscious, and control over my beliefs. And I can use them as tools to achieve the unimaginable.

When I began applying that knowledge to my everyday life, I started seeing results, far beyond what I could have ever hoped for. Now I know, I really do, that you, too, can do the same. This is *WHEN* you put in the effort. That is what life is all about, isn't it? *What you "put out" there, is what you "get back"!* It sounds simple. But think about it. As Tesla pointed out, the universe is energy, frequency, and vibration, including humans. What vibrations you put forth, the energy you share within your environment, influences you in ways you never realized.

How many of you have ever cooked your favorite, most tried and true recipe when either upset, in a rush, or stressed out? Then you learn, surprised via tasting, that your meal is utterly and ghastly inedible or just not as delicious as you know you've made it. Why do you think this is happening? It is due to the vibrations you emit into the universe.

When my kids tell me after I make dinner, "Mom, this taste so good!" and I'm like, "Really? I made it the same as I always do." But sometimes it just tastes a bit better than before. I always tell them what my mom used to tell me, and continues to tell me, "I made it with love!" I used to think this was a joke but later realized how true it is. For anything in life what you do with love will reflect in your work. On the flip side however, when I have felt rushed to make dinner (one too many times!), that created stress on me and dinner was not my best.

And hence your stress, sadness, and discontent create an energetic resonance within your environment, which in turn reflect back upon you, amplifying and perpetuating these negative emotions. Remember my friend who thinks all guys are jerks? Her past relationship disappointments have left her in a state of emotional disharmony, creating a frequency vibration that attracts and manifests experiences that mirror her internal state. This phenomenon suggests that our thoughts and emotions influence the experiences we attract into our lives. The universe, in essence, reflects, delivers… and re-delivers!

Now, imagine where else this may show up in your life? For example, I am sure you have personally experienced the perception that you have started your day on the so-called "wrong foot." When you say this to yourself, do you notice how the rest of your day turns out? It's in line with the saying, "When it rains, it pours!" It's not so much about how big the problem is, but how you deal with it. Your reaction will determine what happens next. Why? The energy you exude into the universe is why. The reaction comes with a "vibrational energy." Reactions have consequences.

Our thoughts are electrical impulses that produce specific brain wave patterns. Your thoughts give you a level of vibrational energy. I know this is a lot! Stay with me while I geek out on you on neuroscience/neuroplasticity, God's creation of our brains and the universe! My absolute top favorite topics! When thinking of a bad situation, or a negative thought, that awakens a vibrational energy that produces a corresponding frequency in the quantum energetic field, where all energies (good or bad) interconnect. This is how we manifest. Your consistent frequencies can attract that same energy, because it's the case of "like attracting like."

Our feelings and emotions all have consequences, so if you are emitting a frequency of constant worry, you will likely attract other similar circumstances toward you, because it has to match that energy. You've now been made aware, so, choose wisely. Get mad, yell! Get it out. Then, move on. Change that frequency! Because that frequency has a destination and every destination has a result of potential destruction; if you don't interrupt it, that is. However, you aren't doomed because you reacted poorly at first. Get this—the negative emotions, "your reaction," your fearful thoughts, etc., all emit at a much lower frequency compared to that of a positive energy of thought. This helps you by giving you time to "change the channel"! This switch can be done as easily as simply saying, "There are bigger problems in life, thank God this isn't one of them." This will automatically change your vibration.

I'm not saying that what you are experiencing may not feel like it is the worst challenge of your life. Or that you have to sit there and be delusional about the challenge that you're facing. (Although it doesn't hurt if you do.) But simply being aware that you can potentially be making it worse is key. And that you can indeed do your part to go through the storm in a more productive way, one that will help you versus sabotage you. But now imagine if instead you changed your vibrational energy to hope or gratitude; and yes during the storm, small or big. You've now changed that frequency and to a much faster frequency at that! Now, imagine what that vibration will bring to you? Life will in turn bring you something better, even if it's just simple calmness, enough to get you through with grace, which will produce a better outcome.

And guess who gets to determine when to change the vibrational energy? You do! No one else gets to determine that for you. Not your mom, not your kids, co-workers, clients, not even your partner—it's all on YOU! Your attitude—whether you feel frustrated, defeated, or positive—will really impact how things turn out. You are responsible for managing your emotions, even when it seems hard. I've been there. It doesn't mean you are a robot lacking emotions; it just means that when you know it is not serving you and that it has consequences that you are mindful to change what is not serving you. It is not about being perfect; I lose my shit and I yell at times! But I choose not to dwell on that vibrational energy. I check myself; I focus on what I can control—my inner thoughts to move me toward what I want instead. So, don't let perfection consume you; what matters most is how quickly you can change your attitude to a vibrational energy that will benefit your outcome or at the very least increase your chances!

Depending on the stage of life you are celebrating, we can easily misread the signals we emit when faced with circumstances that affect us, positively or negatively. There are false beliefs that are easy to spot upon reflection. Sometimes looking back on our childhood beliefs, from the perspective of an adult, we can fascinate, amaze, surprise, even laugh at ourselves. How could we have believed something so blatantly wrong our entire lives? (No, swallowing your gum won't stay in your stomach for seven years!) Other realizations can take much longer though. Those journeys might be painful to walk through at times. Sometimes we may refuse to accept and believe what we are witnessing on this reflective walk. Other times we welcome them with open arms.

I know we've just started this journey together. But I promise you, this book will help you to get there (consider it an "owner's manual"). It's not because I am a scientist in the world of quantum physics, or because I have discovered a magical cure-all for ailments of the body and soul. And I'm certainly not a pastor either. It's because I am a person who is just like you, who has walked through the fire before you, and returned as a phoenix with the grace of God, building myself up from the ashes of my past for a bright future filled with endless possibilities, and a life rich with purpose and meaning.

That is why I know within the deepest parts of my being that you can do it, too, because I did it. I still do it. We all struggle at times; we all have questions; we all want to feel loved, accepted, and living a life of meaning. I also have been in the trenches of self-doubt. Believe me. I was a "master manifester" of what I didn't want. And someone who was also blindingly oblivious and naive to have the sensibilities to know that I was stuck in a vicious cycle, courtesy of my own doing, decisions, beliefs, attitude, and behaviors. It was an amazing feeling when I finally realized that nothing will change as long as I keep repeating the same mistake! And the only things I'll attract are the circumstances opposite to what I truly want. How simple yet profoundly illuminating!

We as humans are created absolutely perfect. You are a perfect creation from our perfect Creator, even with your imperfections. The universe is created to exist in perfect balance, in unison of vibration that plays a symphony of emotion. And we are in the center of it. This is the moment where you have the power to choose. Not tomorrow; not on Monday; not when you don't have little work on your schedule; not when the kids move out; not even when you have the perfect running outfit.

Now.

In this pivotal moment, right now, you possess the agency to make a conscious choice and embark on a new path. Regardless of your background or circumstances, you are inherently equal to any individual deemed powerful, strong, and successful. We are all fundamentally interconnected, sharing the same human experience, emotions, and potential for growth. You have the inherent capacity to achieve greatness, just as any other individual does, including myself. Choose this clean slate.

Pushing and Pulling Through

I was a child who was raised in an unstable environment, became a teenage mom, single and fighting her way out of a psychologically destructive marriage by the time I was in my 20s, and fighting for her children's future. I have lived it. And this is why I believe… No! I KNOW within my heart that YOU, yes you, can also break the cycle and push and pull your way through to the other side.

We either personally know or have seen successful people doing amazing things or what we call *winning at life*. These titans seem to have it all. Everything is picture-perfect on the outside—the success, the money, sometimes the fame, the cars, the great family, the vacations. You name it. This is what we see from our vantage point. Take note, this is just the "front of the picture!" What you are unaware of is the "back of the picture," what it took to get there. Or how inwardly broken they were. You don't see the struggles, the sweat, and tears shed in order to succeed. Strange to say, but true, it's the struggles—specifically, how we respond to them—that shape us in the most beautiful way possible. Often it is through our struggles that we reach our full potential. Your pain right now will become your power tomorrow ... This I promise you. We often feel like we're alone with these challenges or insecurities; yet there is a woman or man, just like you, in this very moment, going through the same experiences you are. I remember before starting my journey as a coach and speaker. I experienced a breaking point. I was on my knees asking God for grace, I heard a voice saying to me, 'this is not in vain.' I knew right away, that the reason for my pain, the reason it felt "hard" was because of what God was preparing me for ... a greater purpose, yearning inside of me. My calling was so much bigger than my pain. I knew I had to break through, not only for my kids, but for me, and the future of who I was becoming. That's where my purpose was born. I want you to remember this when you feel life is *hard*. *I want you to tell yourself,* "*My calling is bigger than this pain.*"

People who are truly focused on not just changing but transforming their circumstances commit to the universe created by God, in attitude and vibration, resonating from every fiber of their being, that they'll allow nothing to stop them. I want that for you. As we discussed I want you to know that you have the power to control your thoughts, to redirect them by *"changing the channel"* and to build new ones that will get you whatever you want from life and take you wherever you choose to go.

I know you picked up this book because you are yearning for better answers. Maybe you feel lost, or don't know where to begin, and you want to know *how* to do better, be better, live better, or you want to go bigger and be bolder! Or maybe you are just curious and want to understand why certain patterns keep repeating in your life, feelings of self-doubt, feeling as if you can't free yourself from the treadmill of life. All the way to juggling responsibilities, families, jobs, children, societal expectations, and your emotions—simultaneously. Some of you might be on the cusp of searching for answers to existential concerns such as how to start something new, how to clutch that desire you've long yearned for. How do you bring into existence your life's purpose?

You can achieve anything that you can imagine, and even more, when you live your life devoid of self-imposed limitations. Scientific research has now confirmed that belief in oneself significantly improves the likelihood of success. Sure, life can catch you off guard with unexpected surprises, restrain your movement, and blind you as you are progressing. It can seem hard to see the light at the end of the tunnel at times. But as the adage goes, "even in darkness you can still see the stars!" The light is always there for you to move toward. Otherwise, the feeling of defeat will be upon you.

I loved to run when I was in sixth grade. The feeling of freedom, the feeling that all my worries, sorrow, hardships, and heartbreak were behind me. I was running. And with every tap of my ponytail on my back, I felt the acknowledgment of my inner self, of how awesome I was at it. I was swift and competitive. I oozed confidence. My speed intimidated my classmate competitors. My success in Track and Field gave me a taste of competition and the pleasure of winning. These experiences I carried with me later into the business world.

I remember winning a race. I crushed it. A co-ed one at that! Pride consumed me. It was such a great feeling. I was proud of myself. After the race was over, my PE teacher approached, as if to congratulate me. He put his hand on my shoulder, lowered his face so our eyes equally met.

"How do you think you did, Diana?" he asked me.

"I won the race. I was very fast," I answered, catching my breath.

"Did you?" he said as he intensely gazed at me. "Did you win the race? Or did you just not lose it?"

This confused the heck out of me. My coach further continued and uttered something so powerful that it altered my perspective and stayed with me to this day!

"Diana," my coach said. *"You are very fast indeed. You are much faster than you even think you are. That is why it pains me so much when you run like this."*

I felt my lower lip trembling. I didn't understand what I could have done better. I ran as fast as I could… Didn't I? Did I?

"When you are running," he continued. *"You keep looking back to see how far behind the other runners are. This is what is holding you back. You are so consumed on how much faster you are, compared to the other runners, that you lose precious seconds in your run. Achieving the best run that YOU can run doesn't rely on comparing yourself with others. It matters how fast YOU can be. And if you are so focused on how others are doing, you won't outrun yourself."*

From that day on, I never looked back. Years later, I came to appreciate this simple lesson instilled into me by a non-family member during my childhood… the importance of positive beliefs. I realized that I was the gatekeeper of my mind. What I realized at such a young age is to not worry about others, and instead focus on where I am headed, not on what others are doing. I later realized and also learned that I only have to worry about what I can control versus what I cannot control. I am responsible for the thoughts I allow to enter; this includes what I also choose to reject. My thoughts as a runner in school were mostly fears of losing the race. It is up to me to decide if a certain vibration is bringing a positive or negative change within me or my circumstances.

You, too, are the gatekeeper of your mind. You ultimately decide how much weight you give to others' opinions and how they impact you. The question that I have for you is, are you ready for that? Are you ready for a breakthrough to take you to a new level? Are you ready to shed what is dragging you down, restraining you from moving forward?

Are you ready to question what you've always believed as true and open the door to uncover new possibilities? And rebuild yourself in a way that will bring your utmost desires to the surface and help you achieve your goals? Are you ready to 'change the channel' and change the rest of your life, with more faith, more confidence and live up to your *true* God given potential?

I thought so.

Let's go!

"For as he thinks in his heart, so is he."

—Proverbs 23:7

CHAPTER 2

The Power to Make a New Choice

"Would you tell me, please, which way I ought to go from here?"

"That depends a good deal on where you want to get to," said the Cat.

"I don't much care where –" said Alice.

"Then it doesn't matter which way you go," said the Cat.

"– so long as I get SOMEWHERE," Alice added as an explanation.

"Oh, you're sure to do that," said the Cat, "if you only walk long enough."

—Lewis Carroll, *Alice in Wonderland*

At trainings and events I attend as a keynote speaker, I often hear people say, *"There is nothing I can do about my situation."* This mantra is like hearing nails on a chalkboard. (Do you remember that chalkboard?) It truly breaks my heart. Unlike most other false beliefs, though, this can seem like it is the most challenging to change, especially when you are in the depths of what it is you are experiencing. Why? People often believe that there is nothing they can do to change it. They're too caught up with what they perceive as being their reality. This could not be further from the truth.

Hardship, or the environment around you, can instill the notion that you have no control over your destiny, and that you aren't participating in events occurring in your life. I understand how those false beliefs are born. I had them, too. There was a period when I felt incapable of making new life choices. I lacked the awareness and even energy to *"look for something more"* and alter the course of my environmental circumstances. But here is the curious thing: These accumulated moments (and there were many) blended into a blur, forcing me to question my power, my strength, and my future. I felt the desperation of a single moment daily, oftentimes several times a day. However, the mind is a powerful instrument. Its primary directive is to protect its host—YOU! Those instances of tribulations are now hidden in the fog of memory, veiled in the shroud of the distant past. You still are aware those experiences occurred; but your mind considers it irrelevant now. You choose where to place your attention. What I do clearly remember though is the day I came into my power and made those key life-changing choices, which forever altered the course of my destiny, and my life's purpose.

Make a New Choice

I remember vividly making the inevitable decision to be a single mom. Don't get me wrong; this was brewing for a while. Continuing life with someone I knew wasn't right for me, and certainly wasn't the right example for my kids, was psychologically unhealthy. I would always ask myself, "How will it impact the future of my kids if I stay? What kind of mother would I be?" Sudden, intrusive memories of my parents' incessant fighting would often invade my mind. Although my dad never hurt my mom—physically, that is—I had to endure the yelling, the shouts, and the screams. Putting a pillow over my ears, hoping it would stop proved useless. Nonetheless, I was continuing this cycle as a young adult mom. I broke a promise to myself. And it hurt. Because when I was 14 years old I had vowed that one day when I became a mother, I would never put my kids through the fear and anguish I felt growing up. Fear of losing my mom, fear of what tomorrow would bring.

Although I knew for a long time that this decision must occur, it took courage and all of my inner strength to make this choice. In order for you to have the strength to make a new choice, you have to grasp on to hope, hope for a better way. If you don't have hope, you have nothing.

That is exactly what I did! I saw myself living a better life. I didn't know with whom as a partner, but I envisioned a better life for and with my kids; one that was of greater certainty, peaceful, and in a nurturing healthy environment. I knew I was meant for more. I was meant to live a life different than the one I was living.

A personal conflict in just one area of your life does interfere with other areas. Our domains of activity are interconnected. For those who have been or are currently struggling—with facets of a partnered relationship, intimate or otherwise, or with life in general, or even struggling to start or expand a business—all what I have spoken about, and am about to elaborate on will sound familiar. You wake up every day, thinking "this is the day when things will be different!" See, we've made it through the day without too much drama and unexpected surprises. Everything seems fine. But the harsh reality of dread lurks, residing in your stomach, just biding its time for the opportune moment to strike.

You are trying to convince yourself that this week, this month, this year will be different. You promise yourself you'll take the necessary steps when you set money aside for the kids; you are just waiting for that right higher-paying job to get back on your feet, or waiting until you receive that bonus, or complete that professional training course. There might be tears shed… But you simply and fearfully just can't muster the courage to take the next step. You might even say, "No! When the kids graduate, that's the right time. Definitely."

It's definitely not!

I've been through a myriad of these deluded mental scenarios. I made all the excuses in the world for me being stuck, sticking to where I was in life. I had convinced myself and others why things are the way they are. But deep, deep down, in my heart of hearts, I knew that for me, moving on had to be the next step.

The more I focused on the traumatic images and the present circumstances in my life, the more the tears seem to burn. Burn to the point that they forced me to wipe them away, which I did. It was as if I was clearing a slate and starting anew. At the time, I did not know what I wanted, but I knew what I did not want. Even seeing myself with my kids in a place of calm is what I knew I needed to create.

The Catalyst for Change

My oldest son, now a grown adult, and I were cleaning out our basement, getting rid of unwanted items. It's an innate human habit to hold on to "things" of the past, even when it's no longer needed; or has outlived its purpose. This only takes up space, blocking new opportunities and possibilities. We were looking at what to toss, what to keep, laughing at the memories each object aroused. All of a sudden my son went silent; he just went silent! I turned around to see why. He was staring at a broken picture frame that seemed stuck in his grip.

I, too, went silent. Like all other items in this basement, that broken frame carried a history (the frame I kept procrastinating to repair).

"I remember," my son said.

We both appreciated the mutual silence while staring at the frame. Summoning the courage to change isn't easy for most. But sooner or later a threshold point will make itself known. This is the opportune moment when you see, hear, and/or feel you must change! My ex-husband had flung a bottle at me with the ferocity of a major-league baseball pitcher. I dodged it—barely—still feeling the wind wiz by my right cheek! The bottle crashed against the picture frame, making a profound dent in the middle of it. My son remembered witnessing that when he was 7. This was my threshold moment! I grew up in a home of constant chaos; only when hell freezes, thaws, and freezes again will I repeat the same for my kids!

I have seen this time and again when others, having recently ended an abusive relationship or struggle with some other life circumstance, look back in shame, sometimes in gut-searing humiliation and ask, "How did I let things get so out of control? How did I not make a different choice and do something sooner. How did this become my journey?"

Being in situations that deplete your energy where you feel you were meant for more is never the path you are meant to take, no matter what choices you've made in the past. Making a new choice—now—doesn't immediately guarantee instant change either. But it is definitely the beginning of a change that's about to happen. Each circumstance is unique. Confusion engulfs us at times. It will influence our choices, meaning what decisions and behaviors we choose or refuse to take. Let's face it; figuring out what you want is oftentimes a lot harder than figuring out what you *don't want*. Easier said than done. The Alice in Wonderland quote at the beginning of this chapter sums it up . . .

We all know what makes us feel sad, mad, or hurt. It is human nature to want to dodge such uncomfortable feelings as those. As a matter of fact, avoiding suffering is often used as justification for decision-making. And no, they are not always *good* decisions. The following are pointers to keep in mind . . .

Just because:

- Something is labeled as *"not suffering"* doesn't mean it is happiness.
- You are *"not being hurt"* doesn't mean you are safe.
- *"You haven't lost your temper in a week"* doesn't mean that you have your emotions under control.

In the theater, actors keenly understand that even silence is a form of communication—*"the act of silence is an act of speaking!"* This concept highlights how passive behavior is often a deliberate choice, albeit an unconscious one. When you believe you're "not making an *active* choice," you're still choosing, just not consciously. For example, saying, "I would rather have anything than this," isn't passive; it actively focuses on what you *don't* want, rather than what you *do* want. When I walked away, I wasn't just rejecting my situation; I was actively choosing a different reality. My focus shifted from what I didn't want to what I wanted. This was the new choice I was making.

The Power of Choice is one of the first and vital concepts I teach. For success to occur in any facet of one's life, realizing that you *always* have a choice is paramount—no matter the circumstances! Anyone who calls themselves a human being is as powerful, wise, wholesome, individual, and capable of dynamic life-enhancing decision-making. As difficult as it is to admit, you are responsible for the choices you make for yourself—the good, the bad, and the ugly; this also includes the choices you don't make!

Refusing to make a choice is also a choice. It comes with all of its inherited consequences. Letting yourself be, going with the flow, letting things happen to you, versus proactively taking action with intention to shape the intended course of your life, leads people into the direst of consequences and situations that are difficult to escape. Did you *choose* this behavioral strategy to run your life?

Every choice you make doesn't have to be the right one. That's impossible. We are human. We've all made choices we've regretted, even if you don't care to admit it out loud. Such is life. Whatever choice we make, though, we must remember that we do have a secret weapon that can help us in any circumstance or situation... You don't have to let your circumstance control you. *You can make a new choice.*

You are probably thinking, "This is it? *A new choice?* You've got to be kidding me! If only it were that simple!" I hear you; I see you; and I am telling you, YES! This is exactly it; but note, it is far from always feeling simple. We sometimes are under the notion that it is too late. You made this decision. Now you have to live with it. That it's final. Wrong! You don't have to. You can go again! You can decide now, yes, right now, to make a new choice! It takes a moment, just a moment, to change your life for the better! The darkness is never permanent. Even though your first step will be the hardest, the ones that follow will get easier. In fact, research even confirms that the hardest step is your *first!* And when you take your *first* step, you have a greater probability that you'll take the second step and the third... etc.

In *The 7 Habits of Highly Effective People: Powerful Lessons in Personal Change*, Steven Covey reminds us that "Until a person can say deeply and honestly, 'I am what I am today because of the choices I made yesterday,' that person cannot say, 'I choose otherwise.'" It is a journey. But there is absolutely no circumstance that cannot be changed by our choices. Even if you feel that your body is physically imprisoned, you have a choice in how you will allow this to affect you. Will you rise to the occasion? Or will you crumble under the weight of the circumstances?

Take a moment and think about this. What are the choices you made that you may not feel so proud of that led you to where you are right now? Write them down. Go on, you don't have to feel ashamed. No one has to see it but you. Forgive yourself for the things you may feel ashamed of. It's okay. I used to feel shame, too. It was so freeing when I released it though. This allowed goodness to enter my life.

This letting go of past circumstances that no longer serve you is akin to my son and me cleaning out our basement in order to make space and opportunity for new things. To get you wherever you choose to go and whomever you *choose* to be!

Take, for example, Nick Vujicic. He was born with tetra-amelia syndrome, a rare disorder characterized by the absence of arms and legs. He is a motivational and inspirational speaker, graduated from university, and has a beautiful family. What choices do you think he makes every morning when he wakes up? Do you think his choices were easy to make? Do you think he didn't have to struggle and fight with himself and his circumstances to achieve all that he currently has? Then why not *you*, I ask? Do you feel capable to make a new choice? Do you believe you possess the strength to do it? I will answer for you—every single person is capable of making a new choice. I will prove it to you.

Your Journey

Ancient Chinese philosopher Lao Tzu coined this adage, *"A journey of a thousand miles begins with a single step!"* This is where you begin... with a single step! Let's begin with an exercise:

For a moment, forget about your circumstances. Forget about your past choices. If you could make any choice, any at all, right now, that *will* change your current circumstances or will move you in the direction to achieve your best life, what would that be?

Would you:

- Learn something new?
- Ask for a promotion, the one you aren't sure you are qualified for?
- Start painting because it fills your soul?
- Start that business you've been dreaming of?
- Ask that attractive person out on a date?
- Start exercising to start the journey of getting yourself healthier?
- Call your friend or sibling after bridges were burned?

The list is as long as your journey is. What are your questions? What is it that your heart secretly desires? Take a piece of paper out and write it down. Go on! Take that piece of paper and write it down.

Do it NOW.

Look at what you've written. And if you skipped through the exercise, I know you can think of something, no matter how small it is! You'll thank me later. I promise. (If you're eager to keep reading, you're cheating yourself.)

Now, read your answer to yourself. I want you to *see* the words. *Feel* them for their power, because *words are powerful*! And when combined with the power of your mind, through the mental activity of visualization, you will be... let's just say... unstoppable! In Chapter 9 I go deeper, with visualization, so you're in for a real treat!

Again, you have to BELIEVE in what you want to ACHIEVE. Entertain thoughts that serve you and propel you toward the goal you want to manifest. This is real, and I am not the only one who has seen the power of it. I am not even the first to write about unshakable power. I am just here to tell you that it works. I know because I have experienced it firsthand, and it changed my life. You are the person building your journey through your beliefs. And your beliefs are based on what you (and sometimes others) are telling yourself—repeatedly!

Case examples:

- "I don't have the money to do it right now!"
- "I'm not good enough."
- "Diabetes runs in the family; I will probably get it when I am older."
- "I'm not ready yet."
- "I am too timid."
- "I am not a good cook."
- "They'll laugh at me."

Ruminating on negative thoughts and beliefs imbues them with an undeserved sense of truth. These self-fulfilling prophecies then dictate the course of your life. The negative self-talk mentioned earlier is precisely the obstacle you must overcome through conscious choice. To break this cycle, begin by examining your internal dialogue. For instance, if you aspire to improve your fitness but constantly compare yourself unfavorably to others, berate yourself for perceived shortcomings, and undermine your efforts, how can you realistically achieve your goals?

If you want to scale your business, but you are held back by fear in the shape of negative self-talk, and even imagining things not going well; if you aren't actively making the necessary choices to get you there, how are you going to make that happen? If you are telling yourself that "all men/women are jerks," then how would you expect to make space in your life for a loving and respectful relationship? Your negative self-talk won't allow it. Every thought that you have right now is contributing toward your future—positive or negative.

The more you allow your brain to wander to a place of fear, the more you permit fear to dictate how you feel and, in turn, what direction your life takes. Uncontrolled fear is not to be ignored. Millions of people struggle to overcome it, constantly fighting. But this does not have to be your reality. You are the only person who can keep your narrative alive. I'm not suggesting we should become emotionless robots, devoid of any negative thoughts or fears. These emotions are an inherent part of the human experience. Fear will arise; it's inevitable. There will be times when you're genuinely scared, and those feelings are valid.

We're designed to experience this spectrum of emotions for a reason. Our minds are naturally wired to anticipate potential threats. It's simply how we're built. This ability exists to prompt you to be aware of potential harm that might come your way. Or to anticipate real-life threats/concerns early enough to spark change or plan accordingly. It's okay to plan accordingly but not to manifest it simply because you're planning to be safe. Take, for example, wearing your seatbelt. You wear it to keep you safe in the event there is an accident. Does it mean you should dwell on it and create senseless, fearful thoughts that something will happen? Of course not. You simply do it because you know wearing your seatbelt is likely a good idea. *It's within the security of your preparedness that it's best to have it and not need it than need it and not have it.*

The key is to prevent these negative thoughts from paralyzing you. Yes, acknowledge them; but don't dwell on them. Or they will take flight on their own and start emitting that vibrational energy we talked about in Chapter 1. It is how we manifest things into our existence. There will be instances where these negative thoughts serve a valuable purpose, such as keeping you safe, warning you to pay attention to something.

But I also know that there are more times than not when negative thoughts will bring along self-doubt to restrain you, holding you hostage. The preface of our worry begins with negative "what if . . ." scenarios. Then you make choices and decisions based on what could go wrong instead of on what *could* go right! Why? All because of *fake* fear, the false perception of a scenario that brought you nothing; nothing but missed moments for change. How many times throughout your life do you incessantly worry, only to discover that things turn out okay? How many opportunities do you waste per month? We live in constant worry and anxiety, sometimes going a thousand miles an hour, thinking if we worry hard enough that things will work out in our lives. How many times did you rob yourself of peace because you permitted useless fear and anxiety to take over based on assuming the worst? You can't allow fear of any kind, such as what others might think, to restrain you from doing all of the amazing things that you were born to do!

We evolve as human beings—we're constantly growing and changing. You were never meant to stay the same. That version of you wasn't meant to last. Sometimes we resist change out of fear. But the truth is that the only thing we should truly fear is stagnation. Not changing. Not going for what we want to avoid the pain of rejection. My biggest fear was to one day live in regret. To be that 95-year-old woman wishing I had done the very thing that I felt led to do but didn't. I feared bathing in the regret of missed opportunities. When your mental image is constructed on the foundation of fear, you leave no space for peace and happiness. This mental image will crumble, ruining what could be. What you can control is the here and now!

Most of us have what the acronym F.E.A.R. means:

False

Evidence

Appearing

Real

Let's do an exercise:

Step 1:

Examine the obstacles you face. If you can name all your fears, what would they be? Write them down. Example below.

- Fear of failure
- Fear of rejection
- Fear it won't work out
- Fear that they will judge me
- Fear of making the wrong decision

Step 2:

Now, stay with me on this next one. When you encounter fear, you are neurologically encoding it. What are the moments and events that are associated with this fear experience? Below is an exercise that unravels it all.

- If you had to show me how this fear makes you feel, and what it actually looks like in your mind, how would you do that?

- When you think about this fear, what image do you see in your mind?
  - Is it a picture or a movie that is happening?
  - Is it close up or far away in the distance?
  - What sound does it have? What do you hear?
- Where is this feeling located in your body? (Is it in your stomach, chest, or shoulders?)

Step 3:

What alternative outcome could there be instead? Imagine the following:
- What if you do succeed?
- What if it actually does work out?
- What if this was your breakthrough?
- What if you empowered others by doing this?
- What if they did like you?

Step 4:

Now imagine for a moment that it did work out, where the fear that was holding you back no longer exists, and is now replaced with the opposite of what you feared. Your desired outcome is actually your outcome. What did you replace fear with? Now that you've gotten over that fear, what is it that you have achieved? Now, follow the steps below.

1. Close your eyes and take a deep breath. Inhale slowly and deeply. In for four, hold for four, and release slowly for five. Repeat three times or more. (The idea is to prime your brain to relax a bit before you do this.)
2. What does your ideal outcome look like?
   - Imagine that it is working out. And if it did work out, what would you see right now? Where are you? Who are you with? What's around you?

- What does it sound like?
- What does it now feel like?
- Smell like?

Now, you might be thinking, "What? That's it? This is all I have to do to get over fear?" It's actually quite simple. However, you need to practice it. It's like a muscle that you need to exercise. Play with it. I challenge you to do this and see what you discover. We humans often complicate—no, over-complicate—things at times. And remember, it does not mean that fear will never happen. As I said, it will; fear is part of life. The key is to not allow it to cripple you. By stopping the madness, you can relieve yourself and simply increase your chances of the outcome working out in your favor. It does not have to be scary; it does not have to be painful. Life is meant to be beautiful, even with its imperfections, even when it is messy and feels bumpy. You have to hunger for change. You have to be so hungry that you can almost taste it. Taste it as if you were lost in the forest for days and have just discovered the sweet taste of a waterfall to quench your thirst.

You are always building your desired outcome, good or bad. It is always occurring based on your thoughts. Those thoughts can spring from a limiting belief that causes fear. Or it can come from a positive thought that empowers you with confidence.

To get your desired result, you have to be able to build your journey through channeling your thoughts, like a laser beam, to whatever it is that you want. The only thing to fear is truly fear alone, because only fear can stop you from moving forward and experiencing all that is possible. This is how successful people conquer the unthinkable; they do it anyway, knowing that on the other side there's triumph from having the courage to go through it, and the faith that it will take you somewhere good, even if it is only a lesson to go again and do it differently.

For years, if not decades, I was doing something I loved. I helped people, friends, family members—and customers while I was in real estate and even as an EVP, too—to see past their limitations and to go for what they really wanted to achieve in life, and to refuse to settle for mediocre. But, ironically, those career choices were not my true calling; they were only part of the journey I was meant to live. The desire I had burning inside was to show others how to break the cycle of self-doubt and make their dreams a reality. I had the tools I knew I was meant to share with others. Although the career choices I made brought me immense growth and even more breakthroughs than I ever thought possible, I felt they were preparing me for what was yet to come. I was ready. But I would often second guess myself at times, thinking, "I'm just not ready yet. One day!" Until one day turned into months... then years! Ten years, in fact, until I finally said, "No more. My dreams will no longer sit on a shelf to collect dust!"

Listen to your inner voice; it is always guiding you. We are always being divinely guided. Too many times our inner voice is trying to speak to us, but we ignore it. When we listen, we start to live the life we were meant to live, one unrestrained by mental borders, and light that is bright with endless possibilities. Have you ever felt that voice inside nudging at you to do that thing you keep pushing off? Starting that business or going for that promotion? Do you listen and take action? Or do you flat out ignore it because you don't believe you're good enough? Or like me maybe you keep telling yourself "it's not the right time" and "you'll be ready to do it one day?"

I don't believe God plants these seeds of desire in our hearts if He wasn't planning to fulfill them. He is ready to fulfill all of your hopes and dreams. But it is up to you! You have to respond to your inner voice when it speaks to you. That is God doing something amazing. You'll see talents that you didn't even know you had. Too many people oftentimes ignore their gut feeling, that voice they hear. I know you know what I'm talking about! Your inner voice is there for a reason. It guides you more than you may give it credit for. So, take notice. Being mindful that this inner voice exists allows you to be in a more heightened aware state. Ignoring is at your peril.

Have you ever stopped to think about how you're "making things happen?" We are all constantly making things happen in our lives. The question is, are you focusing more on the HOW versus WHAT? Allow me to explain. Simply showing up is insufficient. Why? Running on autopilot is why, dictated by life's influences, or past habits that are all too tempting to get accustomed to. It's like rolling the dice and hoping it lands where you want it to. We operate on such an unconscious level sometimes not realizing it. Have you ever driven to the same place every morning, maybe a coffee shop, and then maybe on a beautiful weekend, you drive to that same place but you didn't mean to? Oh, this happens too many times to count. You get so accustomed to it that you are literally on auto pilot and forget.

For success to occur conscious intent must be a key ingredient in your pursuit. It will also determine how fast you get there. Adding to this is clarity of purpose. This is paramount. You must have such a vivid vision of your goal that it feels almost tangible, as if you can taste it! Without a clear and compelling vision of your success, how can you expect to achieve it? We've previously spoken about the power of beliefs. And when coupled with clarity of vision and purpose, you'll be a force to be reckoned with. Think about anything you've achieved. Did you lack clarity? Or did you know exactly what you wanted? Chances are you had the right vision.

We have all heard of the Pareto principle, which states that 80% of consequences come from 20% of causes. I apply this to achieving goals too. When you are going after a specific goal in your life, 80% of achieving it is riding on your mindset, and 20% is the actual *how-to*. The *HOW* also matters; *how* you get there, the strategies utilized by you to get from points A (present circumstances) to B (goal state), toward your destination. The *purpose* behind what you're after is also vital. This is your *WHY*, your deeply held emotional reason for doing what you do. When you have a big enough reason, a big enough purpose, it will infuse you with energy; it will also be the fuel reserve needed should you ever experience turbulent times while moving toward your goal.

I always say that it is not the quantity but the *quality* of what we do that matters most. It doesn't matter if the task at hand requires 1 hour or 100 hours to complete; the question is, does it bring you closer to the results you need to achieve your goals? Doing an assessment on what you are actively pursuing will illuminate the path, making sure you are still on track, upholding the right mindset to achieve your goals. Mindset is the most important factor to achieve anything in life. Having an unquestioned belief in your pursuit, and in yourself, improves your performance and likelihood for success. When you hear or read the biographies of people who have and continue to have massive world impact, past and present, they share a single thing in common: They all began with having a vision of accomplishing what they sought. Did you catch that? Let me repeat this: they all "began with having a vision of accomplishing what they sought." Powerful, right?

As we see in Mark 9:23, you cannot achieve what you do not believe is possible for YOU!

This is how you build a new road map to your success—focus on changing your mindset and the success will follow.

Questions to Reflect On

- What mindset are you bringing to the table currently? Is it holding you back or pushing you forward?
- Do you catch yourself asking, "What if it does not work out?" more than telling yourself, "What if I succeed?"
- Do you allow others to hold you back with statements like, "You don't have what it takes to do this?" Or do you acknowledge that you might not have it all figured out, but you can certainly find resources, ask for help, or learn how to accomplish your goal?
- Are you easily discouraged by setbacks or failure, or do you push forward, knowing that all successful people have challenges along the way, but what sets them apart is the will to fight through those challenges?
- Do you believe that you either have what it takes, or you don't, or do you focus on the fact that anyone can be great if only they apply themselves to learn?

When building your road map, you have to consider that there are two categories of people, based on how they face challenges—those who LET things happen to them and those who MAKE things happen and rise above their circumstances. I know because I used to *let* things randomly happen to me, thinking that I had no choice and no agency in the matter of my life. Believe me when I tell you that you, too, *can turn around your current life, no matter how big or small the change you need to make is!* I know you can. And I want you to believe that you can, too.

You never know what you are capable of until you push through and move ahead of challenges, adversity, and circumstances. How you tackle these prepares you for any unexpected tensions that may arise even further ahead. This is where resilience and GRIT are born. These cultivated resources are necessary to push you through life's toughest challenges and take you to and past the finish line. You are only as strong as your weakest moment; that is why building a road map for success is vital, because every choice you make or refuse determines if you make a path to success or a pond of stagnation.

So, how do you build your road map?

Remember our previous assignment above (see Your Journey)? Let's flip it over and write some more.

Your Road Map

1. Write one thing that you value in yourself as a person. (Come on, I know you can do this. If you had to imagine it, what would it say?)
2. Write one statement that proves you believe in yourself and what you are capable of.
3. Write one intention that you want to set to achieve your goal. Even if it is one that you will do today, or weekly.
4. Write one statement that you will read to yourself to motivate you if you encounter a setback.
5. Write one thing that you can do to improve your situation if you don't succeed on the first attempt.

There is a principle in quantum physics known as *retrocausality*, which simply means that the *future* can influence the present (effect *before* cause).

6. If you were to write a letter to your future self, with the retrocausality principle in mind, what would you write? (Think about your future self at 80 or 90?)

For *any goal* that you want to achieve, you need a road map, a starting point to build on. By the way, if you noticed, since the beginning of the book, we have followed a methodical process to achieve goals. YES! You have to:

1. Acknowledge

    Acknowledging what holds you back eliminates its power. This is what we began with. Now that you know *what* and/or *who* they are, you will now hunt them down and silence them every time they appear in an attempt to derail you. You can do this by changing the narrative to something different.

2. Set a Goal

    You then followed with writing down what choice you would make if nothing else was a factor. That is your ultimate goal; this is your destination. This is where you want to be.

3. Exercise Your *Grit*

    We ended with you writing your personal road map on *how* to get to your destination, *how* to pick yourself up along the way, and *how* to be intentional.

While this framework outlines three key steps, the path to success is rarely straightforward. In the following chapters, we will explore not only how to implement this star recipe for success, but also how to overcome the inevitable challenges that arise.

"If you can believe, all things are possible to him who believes"
—*Mark 9:23*

CHAPTER 3

Breathing During the Storm

Dear Reader,

I envisioned you before writing this book. I saw how I could make a real impact for you. I saw who I could best empower with my experience, from all that I learned, first-hand, by going through the storm, enduring it, only to rise like a phoenix. Not because I am built differently than you, because I am not. Not because luck played a role, because it didn't. But because of the very thing that I discovered that lives in all of us. That each of us can be great when we uncover our true potential that has always been there. My drive comes from the *one* central question I kept asking myself, until I finally understood the answer. *Why are some people so successful while others struggle?*

If you are reading this book right now, in this moment, it's for a reason. Maybe one even bigger than you first thought. Whether this is you asking the same question as I did or not, you are in for real answers, real change in how you go through life to step into what's possible and see what and who you can be when you apply the knowledge shared throughout this book. Where you no longer have to hope it happens, but you know it will, just by putting into practice the strategies contained within.

My uncomfortable procrastination amplified the urgency to write this book. Everywhere, I saw reminders of the need for help. Delaying this book felt like a disservice, a neglect of my calling. To be frank, it bordered on being a sin! A sin, as stated in the Bible:

> *". . . if anyone, then,*
> *knows the good they ought to do*
> *and doesn't do it,*
> *it is sin for them . . ."*
>
> —*James 4:17*

This book is designed to transform your life just as that *The Power of Your Subconscious Mind* did mine. I'm offering you mental frameworks and relatable life experiences, from stories of loss, triumph, and the devastating impact of limiting beliefs. My stories serve a purpose, which is to awaken your greatness within. This book does not shy away from wrestling with your doubts, insecurities, and your raging desire for more. I'm driven to provide real tools for change. The blessings I've received, the burning call to write this, are for the transformations awaiting you. It's no accident my book—the first of many—is in your hands.

I understand that when you're going through life and feeling like you're stuck, unfulfilled about some aspect of your life, or even worse in the throes of a crisis, it can feel impossible to counter negative thoughts that aren't serving you. However, I know firsthand that it's possible to overcome *any* challenge that you might be going through right now. Yes, right now, in this moment, perhaps. There are some individuals who are already naturally optimistic and motivated. They may find it easier to implement these principles; yet life is not always a bed of roses and the most positive or optimistic humans still have bad days. We all encounter difficult periods, moments where the weight of our circumstances overwhelms us. These challenges can manifest as debilitating moods, insurmountable obstacles, or even physical ailments.

It's precisely during these times of *perceived* impossibility that we need to explore strategies for navigating adversity. Remember, some of the most remarkable achievements were once deemed impossible... until they were actually accomplished.

It's Okay... Until It's NOT

How many times have you caught yourself so busy, so tired, and so overwhelmed that you say to yourself:

- One day, soon, I will eat healthier.
- I will exercise. Or go to yoga. But I am so tired today.
- In a moment I will stop and take a break. But later.
- I can't do that because I'll be away from the kids. I will do it someday.
- I will ask for help because I am exhausted. But I don't want to seem weak. Or no one will do it like I will.
- I'll organize that messy drawer one day, but not today (you know you have at least one of those).
- I will go and see the doctor for my annual check-up. But I'm too busy with work right now. I'll schedule it for another day.
- Etc. . . .

This pattern endlessly repeats itself. Why do we consistently prioritize the needs of others over our own? Why do we habitually make promises to ourselves, or truthfully stated—lie to ourselves that we'll eventually find the time, knowing deep down that these promises will remain unfulfilled? Could it be because:

- You are too "busy"?
- My family will be "upset"?
- Work is "more important" right now?
- We have "no time"?
- It's "too hard, expensive, or too far away"?
- And my favorite one… *"Because I can't!"*

How many excuses do you entertain, trying to convince yourself that the things you need to prioritize for yourself are unimportant, not as valuable as… well, pretty much everything and everyone else?

WHY?

That's what I thought. We have work to do! I need you to confront the notion that you have no time for yourself, *because* what you do is like driving your car on bald tires, thinking, "Well, I am just driving another week, so it will be okay!" Yeah, it is okay until it is not! And then one day, you have that bill—a mile-long, come knocking on the door to collect—your health, your comfort, your happiness, and, unfortunately, sometimes, your life.

The truth is, how you take care of yourself, what's now called self-care, is not taught in school. It's not even taught in families because, let's face it, how many times have you seen your mom or your grandma stop and care for themselves? Nope, they are all wearing that exhaustion for the "good of the family," like a badge of honor. They are proud of it because we, as women, haven't been taught our own value and worth from the time we were born.

And this is exactly how we end up here and now, as overworked and spent mothers, wives, sisters, and daughters. The expectation to do it all fell on... you guessed it—women! You had to be a worker, a teacher, a nurse, a cook, and much, so much more. Oh, and look fabulous while you do it, too! And for you men who do it all, you get credit, too.

At what point do you STOP? No, seriously! You are subconsciously setting an example for others, modeling the behavior you expect from those within your sphere of influence. You are teaching them what you are willing to tolerate at any given time, be it your children, your business or personal relationships, or even just acquaintances. Let's be honest. We are all guilty of this! It doesn't take a ton of reflection to see that we have, and are indeed contributing to the present circumstances we are mired in. Do you know why? It's because we *aren't* victims of our circumstances. Again, we *create* our opportunities; we make things happen—subjectively good or bad!

As a professional working mom, I have experienced this many, and I mean MANY, times. In the real estate business, I had some customers who were extremely needy. Literally, nothing was ever enough. They called me at all hours of the day and night. There were no boundaries whatsoever. Constantly promoting to my clients that they could reach me at anytime was one way I allowed this personal encroachment on my well-being, a consequence of thinking that I always had to be on!

But then I realized the unexpected impact and concussive collateral damage that lack of boundaries had, not only on myself, but on my family. What was I teaching my kids? In fact, what else were they inferring that could leave a lasting impression into adulthood? Self-prioritizing is vital.

A case in point. On airplanes, we're instructed to secure our own oxygen mask before assisting our children. While this may seem intuitive, the reality is that many women prioritize the needs of others over theirs, even in life-threatening situations. This inherent nurturing instinct often leads us to instinctively care for our children before ourselves.

In the past, I would have undoubtedly prioritized my children's safety over my own. But in order to help my child... I learned that I *first* must have a fully flowing and functional oxygen mask secured.

Without clear boundaries, anything goes. Think about it. You become susceptible to guilt trips and feel obligated to comply with every request, regardless of your own needs. This dynamic isn't limited to client relationships; it extends to our interactions with family as well. I certainly learned this lesson firsthand while navigating the formidable negotiation skills of a five-year-old determined to have some ice cream!

The crucial realization dawned on me: Whenever you find yourself in an uncomfortable or unsatisfying situation with another person, it's time for introspection. While you can't control others' behavior, you always have the power to determine how you react and what you will tolerate—and won't.

Asserting your boundaries is essential. One thing I learned is that you must clearly communicate your limits and expectations because people around you are not mind readers. One mistake we make is to assume that they should just know. Truth is, they do not. Make it crystal clear. Don't apologize for upholding your values, your time, and your energy. When you consistently stand your ground, people will recognize you mean business and respect your boundaries. Before anyone can respect your boundaries, you need to be clear about those boundaries *first*. Unapologetically. This self-respect will undoubtedly lead to a more fulfilling and empowered you.

Speaking of boundaries, I was putting the finishing touches on this book when my youngest asked me if I was going to his baseball game. I had gone to his first game. But this one was one I had to sit out. He fully knows why and has been a big supporter of me writing my book. Both of my boys have been. My son was so understanding that it almost brought me to tears. Allowing your kids to be a part of your journey with full transparency is so important. They become a part of your support system. Sometimes they have the best advice, too! They simply understand more than you may think.

Before we continue, stop and take a deep breath. Not just a shallow inhalation, but a conscious, deep breath. Feel the air filling your lungs, expanding throughout your body, from your toes to the tips of your hair. Close your eyes and inhale deeply, then exhale… slowly. Repeat two or three times if you'd like. Feels good, doesn't it? I say this now, as a reminder that although you are reading this chapter, you can stop no matter what it is you're doing, even if it is only a 30-second break.

Here's a question for you to think about: What is that yearning task that you know needs to be completed? This task is just for YOU. It's something you know will lighten the psychological weight off your shoulders when completed. This task will nourish you, restore inner balance. Or it will just give you that certain peace of mind… just because you finally took care of it. What is this task you can do TODAY, something that requires action NOW? For example:

- Book that doctor's appointment.
- Enroll at the gym.
- Make a list of the things you will eliminate that are causing stress. Even if it is one thing you can delegate, do it!
- Have that courageous conversation with your partner or friend on your new boundaries.
- Make a call right now, ask for help.

Now, imagine what that looks like, having already taken action on something you know would help you tremendously... to feel the load lighten a bit... now that you are taking care of YOU! Perhaps you feel the weight on your shoulder... getting a little lighter because you finally took the action you've been putting off.

Remember the things that are vital for the engine (you) to keep going.

Important: Keep in mind that whatever happens, whatever the outcome, make a promise, and commit to yourself that you will always take the time to stop, breathe, and reflect. Not just now while doing this exercise, but always. It's maintenance you regularly must do.

It's Okay to Not Be Okay

Of course, there are circumstances in life that affect us, no matter who we are, what we do, or how many necessary boundaries we have. Whatever it is, be it being burnt out, experiencing grief, or betrayal, the first thing that you have to remember is that *it is okay not to be okay.* The fact is we are talking about moving toward a positive direction, toward growth and higher expectations of ourselves and boundaries from others. This doesn't mean that everything will be all rainbows and butterflies 24/7, 365.

Yes, things can be bad. Yes, things can be painful. But pain is a part of life. Pain builds resilience. It doesn't mean that the rest of your life has to be painful. No way! It doesn't mean that you are forever condemned to your circumstances. No way! It is a storm you will weather, so long as you remind yourself of these simple, yet profound four words: *"This too shall pass."* Just those words alone offer hope, because whatever you say to yourself will shift your focus. The power of your self-talk is unrivaled; for your mind unquestionably absorbs it as truth. This, in turn, changes your brain's chemistry, influenced by your language and how you frame challenges.

Do you feel like hardship is here to stay? Then it likely will be, or at least feel like forever. Do you feel that there is no solution? Then you'll have a heck of a harder time trying and failing to find a solution, ironically and without fail, each and every time.

I remember that period in my life when I felt I had no control over my feelings. I lost my father and had a miscarriage... within months of each other! The physical and psychological trauma took its toll. Six months later the force of my private horror reached its apex. Then I fell into a pattern of anxiety attacks that left me scarred, scared, and exhausted. I just wanted to be my old self again. I dreaded the unpredictable onset of these overwhelming sensations: my heart racing, my hands clammy with sweat, and the suffocating feeling of the walls closing in. This was entirely new to me, an unfamiliar and terrifying experience. I felt like a wild animal, cornered, ready to fight or flee.

I had an anxiety attack at my son's birthday party. I was standing there, socializing with almost 40 guests at our home. All of a sudden, I remember thinking, "Oh no, not this again." (This was the third occurrence within weeks of each other, and I was done welcoming this hopeless experience.) Without notice, it took hold, possessing me like a demonic entity. To prevent any embarrassment, I removed myself for half an hour, trying to calm myself down.

I ran upstairs to hide in my bedroom. I lay on my bed, trying to breathe deeply through the heart palpitations. Then another dark emotional wave rushed into my head. Another demonic affliction. In essence, I was possessed by panic—I felt so hopeless. A full force of it. I went from feeling fearful to anger. Anger because I felt like I was losing grip of what felt like a struggle for my very soul. Someone was going to lose this fight. I was damned if it was going to be me. I remember feeling like "How dare this thing I was feeling spoil this special day of celebrating my son's birthday, one of my biggest blessings, his arrival onto this Earth? You WILL NOT win this! I will!" I screamed—silently!

I felt resolute in my head. The more I spoke to this physical experience I was feeling, by saying statements that moved me toward victory, and simultaneously breathing deeply, intentionally, even imagining my heart rate rhythmically pulsating back to normal, the more I channeled my anger, the more I felt in control. To silence my mind, I continued to breathe… slowly, counting down silently… pacing each breath… putting spaces in between, slowly… rhythmically. Telling myself, "I am calm cool and collected," over and over again as I took slow deep breaths. It felt like a tennis match that I was determined to win.

I did it! I managed to find the power deep within to breathe through the storm and regain control of myself. I visualized myself calming down. I had this vision so deep that I started to experience the very thing I was imagining. I was beginning to take charge for what was happening inside my head and affecting my body. I was stunned! It was a powerful moment when I realized that I did something I didn't feel was possible. God spoke to me in that moment of fear and hopelessness. I discovered this newfound power tool! I learned how to engage my subconscious to help me achieve other goals. And I know how to breathe through a moment of panic; why was I not using it?

Then it hit me in a much deeper way than ever before… I have the power to stop this! I have the power to go past it. I was in control of myself and my surroundings. I knew how to attract things in my life, and I made a decision to put myself first.

You must do the same! No matter whom you'll disappoint; no matter who fails to respect your boundaries, or refuses to honor them, YOU have to do this for yourself. Your body speaks to you. You better listen. You should honor what it is telling you by giving yourself the care and attention you—and it—*both* deserve.

I learned that while you can't stop or avoid the pain, grief, or loss experienced, what you do have control over is how you react, the mindset that you choose to adopt in real-time, and the intention that you set for yourself. Is it easy? Not always; it may feel painful to do so at times (you are human). But you can, and you will, liberate your mental shackles. Don't get me wrong; I don't think you can just "positive think" your way out of all circumstances. But you can improve the odds by choosing your focus, by changing your channel—of focus! While internal control over our mindset is vital, the external world often undermines our efforts, nowadays through social media, advertising, etc.

It then begs this question: Why do we struggle to recover from setbacks? Why can't we simply dust ourselves off and move forward? Social media often presents an idealized version of reality, portraying lives as effortlessly perfect and joyful. But is this facade genuine? Do these carefully curated online personas truly reflect the complexities of human experience? I say NO! These superficial realities can exacerbate feelings of inadequacy. I ask you, how often have you fallen for this visual deception?

Say it with me—*"It's okay not to be okay! It's okay to be vulnerable; as a matter of fact, it takes courage to do so."* Being able to show your true self, instead of the carefully manufactured version of you, to everyone, especially the ones closest to you, is powerful. It demonstrates strength of character to do so. You are strong! You are capable! See it and believe it! (For some... believe it, first. Then see it!) Neuroscience has confirmed the latter to be even more powerful for personal persuasion!

But why don't we ask for help? What prevents us from doing so? We are not alone! We all have people who love and care about us. More often than not, these people will be our biggest cheerleaders and supporters… if we only allow them! It's not a show of strength to try to carry the world on your shoulders. What requires strength is asking for help before you are forced to your knees, like it happened to me. Trying to be super-woman at all times was not only a disservice to my psyche and my loved ones, it crippled me.

I'm sure you can identify with these life experiences: Apologizing for your kid being in the background of your phone call. Case in point: I would hide underneath my desk, hoping that my kids didn't hear me on the phone and that my client didn't hear my toddlers knocking down my home office door to enter. Oh, did they try! Or apologizing for natural human experiences, such as sickness, or missing an important scheduled event because you simply forgot, constantly in last-minute rushes to make sure you have dinner are some of the clear signs you need to stop, take a breath, look within, and examine the current state of your life and personal essence. One way to do so is to eliminate apologizing for normal and natural human events, moments, and behavior. You are human, after all!

You did nothing wrong. Yes, we cry, we sweat, we swear, sometimes we lose our s-h-i-t, and that is okay! What is not okay, though, is staying there—in that dark and gloomy space where our pain and suffering are tucked neatly away, pretending it doesn't exist. The more you adorn this external facade that you have it all put together, when you *DON'T*, the more it will boil and eventually explode.

Your imperfections aren't flaws; they're the brushstrokes of your individuality. Celebrate them! No one shares your unique life narrative. This is the beauty of your creation—perfect in its own right. A part of the Grand Design! Fall in love with your journey, honor it, stay rooted in your truth, and you'll unlock your full potential—without a doubt. Align with your inner essence and watch as your world transforms. The beauty of life awaits. It always has. Acknowledge your strength, your progress, and the fact that you are singularly YOU! Extend to yourself self-compassion with pure acceptance, as you are.

As previously noted, when people say, "Life isn't fair," it makes me cringe! Yes, we all deal with different issues in our lives. Some of us are given a bit more to carry health-wise, others are given a bit more to carry in regard to personal relationships, and others are carrying financial circumstances a bit more. I get it. I know that sometimes obstacles and circumstances we meet on the path can seem a bit daunting, more than what we may feel we can handle. I believe we were created with a built-in capacity to overcome any challenge presented to us. When you have unshakable certainty that God is working this out regardless of what circumstances you're in, big or small, you will go through it differently. External things do not dictate your peace. Peace follows when you have God in your life. This belief provides you with a sense of strength and resilience in the face of adversity. You are stronger than you think! Adversity acts as the catalyst, awakening and strengthening previously dormant strengths within us. It's through the struggles where faith is born or strengthened. We allow God to work in our lives when we have faith that the work is happening behind the scenes for your greater good. Let go and let God.

Sometimes the biggest breakthroughs in growth arise from the deepest pain or an insurmountable obstacle that forces you to look at things from multiple perspectives or tap into a previously hidden and underutilized strength. Weird as it sounds, these are the opportunities to embrace these challenges, including the accompanying of pain and suffering, as opportunities for personal growth and development. And it starts with unconditional self-love. It is okay to feel that love for yourself.

If you are a parent, or expect to be, hear me: It is our responsibility to teach children how to do that, too! It is vital to show them that the mythological tale of the phoenix is not exactly a myth per se, but truth, in that you CAN pick up the pieces; you CAN rise from the ashes. This is what will influence them for the rest of their lives—remembering how you—their parent—manifested a miracle when dealing with an insurmountable circumstance. You didn't cower and crumble on your bathroom floor, crying. The greatest gift you could ever give your kids is the gift of what having faith in God is all about. It will get them through the toughest of times.

I won't forget my 13-year-old (at the time) daughter's face right after she called 911, because I was hemorrhaging on my bed after my miscarriage. She took my face in her hands, stared into my eyes. Her gaze reached, touched, and stroked my soul.

"Mom, you're going to be okay! Do you hear me," she said. "You're going to be okay!"

She said it so calmly, with such power of conviction, that even if I felt like I was falling apart at that time… she brought me back.

I was so proud of her for her strength, her conviction, and her love. I needed the strength she showed me in that moment, more than I realized. I was always the strong one. I was always helping keep others together. And here she was, holding me together with any ounce of hope she could give me. I took it; I took it all in. It impacted me greatly and even brings tears to my eyes as I write this.

That is why I said you have to share your pain; you have to show your vulnerability; otherwise, children grow up with the notion that life is easy and everything falls into place all the time. They are shielded from the struggle; they are protected from your tears, but at what cost?

The cost of not knowing how to deal with adversity when they encounter it in their life and thinking they are the only poor unfortunate souls this is happening to. That's where the privileged mindset comes in. Or oftentimes the "Why me?" and "Life is not fair" feelings are conceived and start growing. Let them see your struggles and how you overcame them. Let them see the power of having God in their lives. This is HUGE.

Don't allow the victim mentality to rob you of your future growth! Don't allow those moments to be a part of your soul. Never allow them to take root in your psyche. Because if you do, that will defeat you more than you know. You manifest what you believe to be true. If you believe that life isn't fair? Life will present circumstances that validate this belief. And no, it does not mean that everything in life is always hunky dory, or that at times life may "seem" unfair. A simple counter to that could be this mantra, "Although life can sometimes feel unfair, overall, more times than not, life is beautiful. Life is full of surprises... that allow me to grow. I get more wins than I do losses. I know life is full of endless possibilities!"

With God's grace, you, too, can and *will* get past whatever challenges you are presently going through. **God works miracles in your life. Miracles are only born from faith.**

Remember that it can either be YOU and Life "against you" or YOU and Life "for you." No one else can decide that but you!

This bears repeating: Your reality mirrors your output. Pay close attention to your words and intentions. They are the attractors that draw people, places, and things into your life. Even when life seems unjust, you are the architect of your experience. Remember, the greatest strength is gained through the struggle to stand up when facing adversity! This is the force that molds you into what and who you will become. This is how you gain resilience, trusting Our Creator to have your back and pushing forward to success. The successful men and women that we praise and are keen to emulate have gone through hardships, struggles, and failures of some kind. Their secret to success or failure is always founded on how they respond to their situation at hand, and the decision to keep going. Dreams rarely come true without perseverance. The decision to keep pushing forward is the key to achieving more.

Think of Oprah. Pregnant at age 14, she escaped poverty to become one of the biggest icons in public life. Maya Angelou, a sex worker, became one of the greatest poets and civil rights activists of our time. Did you know that Walt Disney was fired for "lack of imagination"? Do you know that more than 30 publishers rejected Stephen King's most successful book? (I bet they are still hurting from that mistake.) Did you know I was rejected more than 30 times before publishing this book!? Colonel Sanders was 62 with $100 to his name when he pitched his idea for fried chicken and got rejected 1,009 times! And so many more stories …

I am sharing these tidbits of information because all of these people started with unfavorable circumstances, experienced struggles, rejections and failures. They now empower others to believe in themselves. That is why these stories are powerful, because humans are beautiful and exceptional. The strength of the human spirit is inspiring. You don't have to be Oprah or Walt Disney to make an impact! You are beautiful as you are; you have all it takes to be happy and successful.

Remember, today, that you are inspiring. So why not inspire those around you? Trina Paulus said that the caterpillar wanted to fly so much that she was willing to give up being a caterpillar. And knowing what metamorphosis caterpillars go through (literally become liquefied primordial soup) to become a beautiful butterfly, it makes sense. The purification of the soul through suffering is what brings blessings, and our response to that makes our dreams come true.

Are you ready to become a butterfly? Are you ready for a metamorphosis?

Build and Boost Your Confidence

Ellen Johnson Sirleaf, Africa's first female president, said that if your dreams don't scare you, they are not big enough. I truly believe that. I challenge myself and the people around me to get out of their comfort zone, to do something that really scares and excites them at the same time.

That doesn't happen solely on pure willpower though; it's not an incidental thing. Confidence is like a winter coat, you have to wear it *every day*, because if you skip it, you will truly feel the cold. That means being proactive. If you don't know where your coat is, you can leave in a hurry, and you can forget it. If your coat isn't ready to wear, or if it is ripped, you simply can't wear it. Being proactive is absolutely the most important thing in filling your confidence tank. You don't forget to drink water because it is a necessity, right? This is how you need to think of confidence. You need to refuel it, build it up to serve you better, and raise you to where you want to go. As Neale Donald Walsch said in one of my favorite books, *Conversations with God*, "Life begins at the end of your comfort zone."

What is it that you want that pushes you out of your comfort zone? Take note; most people never make that leap. Why? Because they doubt themselves; they lack the confidence. And, because as humans, we naturally gravitate toward what feels safe and familiar. The difference between those who win and those who struggle is simple—winners put their trust in their vision, and doubt their fears. If you feel you lack confidence I would ask you, what are you doing EVERY DAY to boost your confidence? And most importantly, what does confidence look like for you? Just think about it; when was the last time you really felt confident? Were you wearing a specific shade of lipstick? (For you men, was it that new, freshly pressed suit you wore?) Did you watch a motivational video before your big presentation? Did you get dressed to the nines and feel powerful, ready for your important meeting? Did you nail that important meeting?

You must hold a pristinely clear vision in your mind of what YOUR confident self looks like. In order to achieve it, you must know what achieving "*it*" also looks like, in the future as if it has already happened. Most people rarely create that clear image of what THEY look like when they are confident. It's always the image of someone else being confident that they are trying to mimic. But to experience confidence, you must see yourself doing it.

Lack of self-esteem is one of the top killers of dreams. You have to do some self-reflection, go inside to do the work, some soul searching, and discover who you are and what makes you tick, so to speak. But most importantly, you have to raise your standards! I simply cannot say this enough: RAISE YOUR STANDARDS. Rise to who you are truly meant to be. Build your confidence so that you can be whatever or whomever you choose to. Don't accept the fear of what might be. A Harvard Business School study found that **confidence matters as much as competence** in performance evaluations. People who possess confidence are more likely to achieve success than those who do not. You see why it is important to invest in you? You got this!

Need a confidence boost? I got you. If you think this is hard to figure out, it's not. Sometimes you have to try a couple of different things to find the right recipe, the correct balance for yourself.

Here are some ideas on how to build and boost your confidence that have worked for me. I'm confident they will for you, too:

Follow through on your goals, the promise you make to yourself (big goals, small goals).

Research confirms that your prefrontal cortex strengthens when you follow through on your goals. Furthermore, self discipline builds. This in turn trains your brain to support you with increased focus and confidence. Even if you commit to waking up an hour earlier, this is still an accomplishment. This simple act is empirical proof to your brain that you are disciplined, that you have the ability to exercise willpower and intention. Furthermore, setting and accomplishing goals creates psychological momentum, in addition to boosting confidence. Those small wins matter! You told yourself you would go for the grilled chicken salad instead of the pasta. You did it! That makes you feel good. Not because you didn't eat the pasta, but because you kept your promise to *yourself!*

Take action toward something… even if it looks messy. Even if it is small.

Just BEGIN. Confidence grows by doing. You should see the first time I started writing this book. Sticky notes, crumbled paper everywhere. But it was a start! Whatever action you are taking it's a forward step toward real change that pushes past your comfort zone. This tells your mind that you made it past your discomfort, and that you can certainly do it again. Everything you do for the second time is so much easier than the first. This practice trains and teaches you to learn to become comfortable with things that are temporarily uncomfortable and even messy or just not perfect.

Monitor your self-talk.

The way you talk to yourself shapes what you feel, what you attract, and what action you take. And without fail, the way you talk to yourself will eventually become your identity. By practicing positive self-talk, you are creating a pattern in your mind, forming new neural pathways that will be easy for your subconscious to follow. *Research shows that when we shift our internal dialogue in a positive direction, it can reduce stress hormones like cortisol and activate the vagus nerve, helping the body relax, the heart rate slow down, and the mind return to a clearer, calmer state.*

Be in a daily state of gratitude.

This is one of my favorites. We'll dedicate an entire chapter to this one. Gratitude has been shown to rewire the brain, increase dopamine and serotonin, and significantly boost overall well-being, resilience, and emotional strength. It soothes your soul and fills your heart. And who lacks confidence when their heart is full? Not possible.

Choose your environment wisely.

Surround yourself with people who support and inspire you. Spend time around winners, and you will become one. You are who you hang around with. These are not just words you heard your mom say when she didn't like your friends; it's real and science shows it. If you want to elevate your life, start by elevating who you spend the most time with. The people you surround yourself with influence your mindset, habits, and even your success. Your brain has mirror neurons that naturally mimic the behaviors and energy of those around you. So, if you're around driven, confident people, you'll start to think and act the same way. And your performance will even improve just by associating yourself with high achievers and people who support you.

Visualize your success for anything you want to achieve.

Think about a time when you felt super good about yourself—maybe it was when you nailed that business meeting or crushed that recipe. Do you remember how you felt in your body? Was it a feeling in your stomach of excitement? How were you speaking? Get as much detail as if you are re-creating this moment now in real time. This is your recipe.

By re-creating those feelings of confidence, you can then apply them to the areas where you want to grow your confidence. The more you practice re-creating that state, the stronger and more natural your confidence becomes.

Visualize it working out. As if you are sitting in a movie theatre... and are watching a movie unfolding... and *you* are on screen as the star... doing whatever it is that you want to manifest. I can tell you that this is the most powerful activity you can do for manifestation and for feeling good. Everything that we experience has previously occurred (in our minds). So remember the importance of visualizing.

Elevate your energy.

Move your body. Dance, do something to get yourself pumped for your day or for that meeting, with intention, and you'll see how your energy shifts. Confidence lives in motion—when you stand tall, breathe deep, and show up with presence, everything changes. Your mood lifts, your focus sharpens, and your energy will be the driver of how you show up. Remember, you are a vibrational energy; give it the energy you want to match it with, and you will attract more of it.

Become your #1 cheerleader.

Confidence starts with becoming your own biggest fan—backing yourself fully, even before the results show up. When you believe in who you are, everything shifts: your posture, your decisions, and the way the world responds to you. Studies show that self-affirmation strengthens neural pathways tied to self-worth and performance under pressure. Celebrating your wins matters, but it's your belief in *you* that fuels the momentum to keep going. Be the voice that cheers you on louder than any doubt.

With confidence, like with everything in life, it's not about the destination; it's about the journey of getting there and who you are becoming. Heartbreak is real, but it is never in vain, and its purpose is to prepare you for the right things to occur in your life; sometimes, it may feel like a long and hard journey. That is why being mentally prepared up front is so important, so that you don't miss the lessons that life imparts. It does this by throwing those curve balls, even the ones that seem hard to bear.

This journey is not about winning a confidence trophy either. It's about pushing yourself to be better, not better than anyone else, but better than you were—yesterday. Doing activities to elevate confidence can feel scary to some. You don't know how things may work out sometimes. But that is where faith comes in! It's about believing when you don't see it yet. Walking in faith and not by sight. You have to see yourself at that end—the destination, being your confident self, accomplishing that goal, and making that change of habit.

Even if you "fail," it's still progress. Failure is merely feedback, guiding your next steps. You've grown, learned, and are no longer the person who didn't try. As the saying goes, "You can't unring the bell!" You can't unlearn what you've gained via experience.

You practiced being confident, you learned about yourself along the way. You gave it your honest and best effort.

It's better to fail at what you try than not try at all. I don't even like to refer to it as "failure." I truly believe that it is only failure if we choose to give up.

No regrets!

"The Lord is my strength and my defense. . ."

—*Exodus 15:2*

CHAPTER 4

Happiness Is Not Something You Seek

This chapter explores happiness as *the* fundamental aspect of the human experience. Feelings of accomplishment and pride are enriching and uplifting emotions as they significantly contribute to our overall happiness. However, it's important to remember that we are the source, meaning we have the power to cultivate a mindset that embraces the beauty and wonder in every aspect of life. Ultimately, happiness is something we *actively* create.

I can hear you in the back of your mind, asking the question: "Well, if happiness is not something you seek, then how do you strive for something better?" That is a fair point, as I know that since birth we have been conditioned to think that happiness is a *thing*, a noun, an unchangeable, fixed event. In other words, akin to an object, something we strive for—outwardly! What that thing depends on is who you are and what your expectations are. Take for example, a lot of high achievers often feel like it's never enough and are still trying to prove themselves. Their worth is about what they do, what they achieve instead of *who* they are. We have to be more do more and we end up becoming our achievements. The issue is not that they want more. Ambition is a gift. The issue is when achievement becomes our identity. That's when you realize success without fulfillment is just another form of emptiness. The moment you separate your identity from your accomplishments, your life changes. You stop chasing validation and start leading from strength. That's when fulfillment stops being something you seek and becomes something you *live!*

But at the end of the day, you "*are aware,*" more than likely since you were a child, that happiness is something you have to work hard for: you have to acquire it, buy it, find it, ask for it, or worse, you must wait for someone else to bring or give it to you.

I disagree. Because I was there once upon a time, chasing happiness with false expectations of what I thought it was. *Happiness is a state of mind*; it is a proactive choice you make, a behavioral activity you practice every day. The happiest people on earth are happy people because they choose to be happy. If your happiness is predicated on the expectations of others or circumstances, this will leave you empty! When external factors are given that much authority, to the point that they dictate your happiness ... that is only short-lived. Worse, it leaves you disappointed, or can even leave you depressed. This is the wrong point of view. I'll reinforce my point, again: Happiness isn't derived from external sources, be that people or objects or what you achieve. Happiness starts from within—YOU! Not from money, titles, awards, or recognition. Yes, those accolades do feel good... but temporarily, as they aren't the source of lasting joy. True happiness comes from knowing your worth, accepting yourself fully, and living in alignment with your values and purpose. God brought you into this universe to make a difference only you can make—living with intention in who you are, how you give, create, and impact others in meaningful ways, and finding the peace that comes from living life on your terms. This is God's intention for each of us.

If you take a moment to really reflect on what's standing in your way of feeling fulfilled, you'll open the door to becoming a new person—from the inside out.

Pay Attention to What You Are Focusing On

How often have you heard: *"I will be happy when I . . ."* *(Fill in the blank)*

- Buy that house
- Make more money
- Have kids
- Get married
- Am healthier
- Lose weight

Do you notice something? These examples all focus on a list of actionable items. While these goals may lead to positive changes, they also suggest that your happiness is contingent upon external factors such as the actions of others, financial security, appearance, or achieving specific desires. In other words, external circumstances dictate your contentment rather than springing from an internal sense of well-being. Furthermore, your attention appears to be primarily directed toward future outcomes. You're envisioning a future state where you possess what you desire and embody your ideal self. However, by fixating on this distant and somewhat uncertain future outcome, you may neglect, fail to appreciate, and miss the treasures of the present moment.

I get it. It is okay to not want to stay where you are if you are discontented, and wanting more. It's okay to lust after your dream car or house. It's okay to want that Louis Vuitton bag. It's okay to desire the love of your life who is destined just for you. It's okay to strive, have ambition, want for a better quality of life, whether that means to be healthier or look better, etc. There's no question that it is absolutely necessary to have a crystal-clear picture in your mind. (Bear with me. I dedicate an entire chapter to that.) But as mentioned this is not what this chapter is about.

Never place conditions on your happiness.
For example:

- "I am barely making ends meet, so I can't be happy because I need more money."
- "When I finally make the time to do that thing that makes me happy, I'll be happy."
- "I feel so overweight; I am undesirable, so I can't be happy; I need to lose weight."
- "When I feel more confident, I'll be happy."
- "I'll be happy again when I achieve that next big thing."

Constant narratives you feed your mind, or self-criticism, even over minor details, can significantly impact your overall happiness. By dwelling on perceived flaws, you may unknowingly prevent yourself from fully appreciating and enjoying the present moment. This constant negative narrative can create a barrier between your current state of well-being and your aspirations for a better future. Essentially, your actions have consequences. Your thoughts and behaviors can either uplift or diminish your sense of self-worth and overall happiness.

Being happy in the moment, with what you have, and your present station in life, doesn't mean you can't strive for more. On the contrary, you should! You should want to accomplish more.

Progression in your goals brings real fulfillment. You should want to be a better version of you. However, it doesn't mean that you must reject the value of what you *already* have.

So how do you build on that? How do you change your conditioned subconscious to see and feel happiness, while simultaneously working toward your dreams? *By focusing on the right things; by listening and speaking to your heart.*

You are teaching your mind to accept the feeling of happiness and its validity as you strive for success in other areas of your life. If you are struggling in your business, not feeling well, or are not yet where you want to be, you can STILL focus on what is going right for you.

Cultivating happiness begins with a conscious decision. This proactive choice sets the stage for a happier life. Start by appreciating the little things that bring you joy. Reflect on an area of your life that fills your heart with joy, whether it's hugging your kids, enjoying your work, your hobbies or your faith, or nurturing meaningful relationships. Identify the specific aspects of these experiences that bring you the *most* joy. Pay attention to the positive emotions that are awakened. True happiness arises from within. When you focus on cultivating inner joy and gratitude, you'll find that external validation and material possessions become less significant. The pursuit of happiness through external means can be a lifelong and ultimately unsatisfying endeavor.

What can you be grateful for right now, in this moment? It can be as simple as:

- Waking up today
- Your health
- Your kids' health
- The sun shining outside
- Tomorrow is a new day
- You still have your mom or dad

We often overlook things we consider simple. I know you can think of a list of things that you can genuinely feel gratitude for. Maybe you're not where you want to be, but can you express gratitude for where you are, knowing that perhaps things can be worse? For example, when I wanted to move to my first house, I would say I am so grateful that I had the opportunity to build memories in my two-bedroom rental with my kids. And I will cherish those memories forever. I was still striving for more. But I was also acknowledging where I was with genuine gratitude. What you desire for your future needs a motivating propellant. Let it be the feeling of gratitude to catapult you into the next level. I knew one day I would move out of that apartment and buy a house. It happened much quicker because of the energy I was already investing into it.

I am not saying you have to be that happy-go-lucky person, constantly exuding a kumbaya attitude, when in reality you may feel unhappy at a particular point in time. All I am saying is you have to change the channel that you're focused on no matter your current predicament. This separates amateurs from rock stars. Changing your channel of focus allows for the right energy and frequency to flow—for you!

We'll talk about negative thoughts later in the chapter because they don't have the final say. But now is the time to talk about positive thoughts and how to grow and nurture them.

Pruning the bad is just as important as watering the good. You won't be happy tomorrow. You'll be happy today. Choose it! Feel it! Share it! No matter what life brings to you. This is YOUR life; the people in it whom you love, and who love you; these are the things that are worth your happiness that make your soul sing.

Embrace what you have in this moment, because happiness lives in you every day, from the moment you awake, to the moment you fall asleep. Shout to the universe that which you are grateful for so it hears you (it's listening) and can bring you even more things you truly want and value, the things that make you happy. I do this every time and it brings me more of what I desire. I challenge you to do the same. This works. It's not just a fantastical story. The universe is reciprocal. You receive that which you give... with gratitude enveloped in genuine feelings and emotions.

Gratitude is a state of mind. You cannot play in this state while simultaneously entertaining states of fear or doubt! It's impossible. Let me be clear. Having gratitude as an agent on your side gives you the advantage for success; however, it doesn't protect you from the inevitable unpredictable fluctuations in life itself that can often feel like a game of roulette.

Sometimes we are dealt a disappointing hand. Believe me, I know. I've had more than one under my belt. Such as the time I opened a clothing boutique store (I love fashion!) and closed it down after having it open for less than a year. Or when I lost my real estate portfolio that I was proud of building. I remember when I first embarked on being an investor in real estate. I had made investors a lot of money. I found them the best deals, I created real estate development opportunities for them, that proved successful. So, I thought, why not me? So, I went out to build my real estate portfolio. I had three properties; I was on fire. I put a deposit down on a fourth property, then I lost it all. The market crashed, and I lost $50,000. Gone. Then I had to sell my other rental properties as well. Cut my losses. It hurt.

What felt deeply fulfilling turned into an absolute mess. To witness something I chose to create flourish and take on a life of its own was an incredible testament to the power of intention and the unexpected beauty of the creative process, from a seed of an idea to it manifesting into reality. I poured my soul and time into it. But like a deck of cards, life happens. I had to make a very tough choice to sell all my properties. In fact, one even sold as a short sale. I knew it was the right thing to do at the time. And I was happy. Why, you might ask?

I was happy—and grateful—because:

- I was making the *right* decision for ME, versus fighting against the current.
- I learned a lot of lessons and met amazing people in my journey.
- I did something that most people thought was outrageous and were scared to do, yet I DID IT!
- I didn't live life worrying about "what if...," I knew the risk involved.
- My kids were healthy which is always the perspective that changes everything.
- I learned invaluable lessons that helped me do better in the future and be more successful. Even when risks don't work out, they often lead you to a better path.

You can't outsource your happiness to external conditional factors. Your happiness is within YOU and you only. You make it. Although I experienced what most call "failure," I chose to be happy even with the simple fact, that I can go again. It's never over.

There is this silly meme that shows two stick figures next to each other, one looking forlorn and the other one holding a huge bucket full of hearts.

"What is that?" the first stick figure asks.

"Happiness," the second figure answers.

"Where did you get it from?" the first stick figure asks. "I looked everywhere, and I couldn't find any."

"I made it myself," the second figure replies.

Silly but true. You are the creator, master, and architect of your happiness. Adding to this, you'll attract even more happiness based on appreciating the existing happiness you already have awakened—now. You must use what you have now as a trampoline to boost yourself toward what it is you want to achieve in the future. Just as finding your passion *is an important part* of this process, so, too, is understanding that personal creation, of using the "now" to build the future, directly impacts how we interact with and interpret our environment, including the runaway popularity of social media.

Social media often receives criticism for its potential to foster feelings of inadequacy and comparison. However, it also possesses dynamic potential for inspiration, learning, and personal growth. The secret lies in our perspective. Just as with any tool or technology, social media can be used for both positive and negative purposes. It's ultimately up to us (you) to cultivate a mindful and critical approach to its use. The late mindset coach and spiritual guru, Dr. Wayne Dyer, popularized this saying, *"When you change the way you look at things, the things you look at change!"*

I love seeing when people put themselves out there, creatively expressing their passions, regardless of the medium they use. Gone are the days when in order to share your creativity to the world you had to either be a titan of industry or associated with a billion-dollar company. Do you want to talk about how you created a greenhouse from scratch? Great! Show it to the world. Share it and inspire someone who hasn't yet done it but wants to. The other thing that brings me immense joy is to hear how my podcast episodes, social media posts, or my live events have inspired others and even positively impacted their lives. I firmly believe that everyone should pursue something that ignites their passion, whether it's a long-held dream or simply an opportunity to explore a newfound curiosity.

Your skill level, whether you're a seasoned pro or a novice, doesn't dictate your ability to create. Go for it! Just do it! Banish excuses and embrace the journey. Discover your passions.

You don't need a complete road map; start with curiosity and see where it leads. Uncover hidden passions by simply taking the first step. Explore the possibilities! I remember telling myself, "One day I'll do it." For 10 years I kept hitting snooze on something that kept calling my name, and I am finally doing what I am passionate about. It changed my life! And I so want this feeling for you too! When I stopped snoozing my passion of showing others how they too can change their lives, it felt like I was living my true calling because I was finally in full alignment with my purpose. I went into my coaching career knowing I would help others change their lives but what I felt humbled to later realize is that it continues to change mine as well. If you always wanted to fly a plane, take a lesson! If you want to start that business, do it! If you want to teach people how you became successful because you have a passion for your work, then share it with the world to inspire others too.

Questions to Ponder:
- What is it that you want to do but you have kept pushing off? Something that you wish you could do. Or maybe pick up where you left off because you gave up and allowed fear to take over. It's never too late.
- What are you passionate about?
- What is something that you want to do all day if you could?

For the answers above I want you to say them aloud, so you can *hear* yourself and the words leaving your mouth. *Feel* those words. Notice what you feel? Did it bring a smile to your face? Did it create even an ounce of excitement?

Note: You might think that the words you tell yourself and how you talk to yourself have no real impact. Well, I'm here to tell you that they absolutely do. (Hence why I included it in your confidence booster exercise in the previous chapter.) Words do have impact; to be specific, words and *vocal tone*.

William W. Purkey said, *"You've gotta dance like there's nobody watching; love like you'll never be hurt; sing like there's nobody listening; and live like it's heaven on earth."* Bah, I say! Dance like EVERYONE's watching! Be proud of who you are and what you can share! You have a gift, a gift that came from God. You CAN inspire others! Create so you can bring happiness into your life as well as theirs, too. Lead by being the living example of what's possible!

For more than a decade, I neglected that little voice inside telling me to pursue my passion, letting it languish like a forgotten treasure. But I finally *chose* to break free from that limiting reality. If something deeply resonates with you, if it calls to your soul, constantly nudging it, then it's your purpose. That flame of desire that keeps burning inside of you is there for a reason. When you start living your life in accordance with what you feel called to do, true alignment occurs. You synchronize not only with your calling but with your destiny. And this my friend is where true happiness lies. Living your life as you were always meant to.

Don't ignore this internal urge! It is not by accident that you feel it; it is part of the plan to get you to take action. Create your own happiness; you've been given the most precious gift of all from God—life. One where you are always being divinely guided. Don't squander it! Embrace it! Walk in faith.

Countering Negative Thoughts

Persistent negative emotions aren't always rooted in imagined fears. Past traumatic experiences can leave lasting imprints on your mind... and in your body. Research led by renowned pain expert Terence Coderre has demonstrated that the nervous system retains "memory traces" of pain. These neural pathways can amplify previously ingrained discomfort, making even minor setbacks feel dangerously overwhelming. This phenomenon is similar to phantom limb pain experienced by amputees, highlighting the profound impact of stored pain memories. Even the memory of pain can activate physical pain. How incredible is that?

Engaging with negative thoughts and images strengthens the established neural pathways that you've created via repeated focus on these unhealthy states, emotions, thoughts, and images. This can lead to an exaggerated emotional response to even minor challenges, potentially triggering feelings of depression and anxiety. Research supports that a lot of our negative thoughts aren't facts—they're assumptions, habits of thinking that distort reality. These patterns often lead individuals to interpret situations in unbalanced, upsetting ways without examining the actual evidence at hand. Left unchecked, they twist how we see situations and leave us feeling frustrated or anxious. Psychologists call these *automatic negative thoughts*, or ANTs. The good news? Once you recognize them and challenge them, you take back control of your mind and your well-being.

When you sustain a thought for more than a few seconds, you are *actively* keeping it alive—by choice. Furthermore, having negative emotions is a part of the human experience. Everyone has them. They do not discriminate. What is even more assuring is that most negative thoughts are assumptions, not facts. Even Mother Teresa grappled with feelings such as doubt and lack of faith. However, she did not allow herself to stay there with that self-sabotaging defeat.

It bears repeating: The crucial factor lies not in the presence of these emotions, but in *how* we choose to respond to them. Our mind possesses immense power. By consciously choosing to counter negative thoughts that do not serve you and avoid dwelling on them, you can break free from the cycle of self-sabotage and cultivate what motivation psychologist Carol Dweck calls a "resilient mindset."

Having said all that I must illuminate this fact: As humans we are hard-wired to sort for what can go wrong. This is how God created all of us. We all have the same exact wiring when we emerged from our mother's womb. This ensures that the biological prime directive is achieved—which is to survive by avoiding any possible hints of danger. Despite this built-in early-warning system, we humans will experience moments and events when so-called negative incidents occur in our lives. This includes negative thoughts, too. It's inescapable. And remember, negative thoughts speak to us if we listen without being crippled by them. They often come with hidden messages. We have certain fears that serve us so we can make a new choice. This attention on avoidance is a powerful force, so much that it distracts us from focusing on contentment of mind, body, spirit, and emotions, which are what we ultimately are striving for.

The good news is that you can "change the channel" to one that's empowering. This is what this book and my movement are truly all about—to get you to experience more of what you want and less of what you don't want. To go through life with more control over your life. If you don't "change the channel," then what's the alternative? (I'm sure you know the answer!) You need to learn to manage your state of mind, or you will self-sabotage. I constantly remind my students, listeners, and viewers of this: "Tell me what your thoughts are, and I will tell you how you're feeling." Whenever a self-defeating thought arises and creates anxiety, or builds a negative landscape of possible scenario outcomes, counter it with a positive thought, just as easily as you would change the channel on your TV. It will change your focus immediately.

Absorbing anxiety-inducing content streaming from a scary channel has a detrimental impact on your emotional well-being. The best thing to do is to "change the channel." Change it to one that streams healthy content, makes you smile, allows you to calmly breathe, and instills hope because you can see the light at the end of the tunnel—that attractive signal from your future. This alone will calm the storm you feel at those crucial moments. It takes a moment to break the cycle; just the same as [a moment] it takes to keep the feelings that hurt you alive. It just takes a moment to put it to bed… or show it the door. Dark and gray are never forever.

We all know that with any storm, a rainbow awaits afterward, accompanied by beautiful sunshine. *The storm had a purpose, and the rainbow is the proof.* Embrace this attitude as if you know, beyond the edges of doubt, that tomorrow the sun will rise and brilliantly shine! Adopt the mindset that even when it is cloudy and stormy outside, "this too shall pass." It's like a rollercoaster where you hold on tight, but you know it will be over soon. When you consciously practice training your mind to counter negative thoughts, you will quickly surprise yourself that you are now doing it automatically… subconsciously. It becomes a habit that's now second nature to you. The more you practice this, the less thoughts you'll have of self-sabotage.

Before we practice replacing thoughts, here is a quick demonstration exercise to experience the power of your mind.

Try something simple, like putting your hand under cold running water and actively overcoming the cold sensation. Vividly imagine a heater warming your hand. Don't imagine it, do it! Experience how it feels. Can you feel the cold water changing temperature? It's not magic; it's simply science—the science of your mind and just how powerful it is. I remember as a kid my mom had me lie down, close my eyes, take a few deep breaths, and imagine a juicy lime cut in half. She continued by telling me to open my mouth and stick my tongue out (with my eyes closed). Then she had me imagine that she was squeezing lime juice on my tongue. I felt that sour sensation in my mouth and even remember feeling the sensation right under my tongue. It was incredible!

Exercise

Turn those negative thoughts around. Here are some scenarios of it in action.

Scenario: You're about to send a proposal to a potential client. You hesitate to set your price at the level you know it's worth because you worry they'll go elsewhere.

Negative thought: "I can't charge these prices—people won't pay that."

Replace it with: "The right clients pay for the value I bring. I get clients who see my worth."

Scenario: You have been preparing healthy meals for you and your family. In addition, your goal is to shed a few unwanted pounds. However, something unexpectedly came up at the last minute making you late for preparing dinner. You now have to abandon all plans for dinner and order pizza.

Negative thought: "I am not doing a good job managing the healthy eating habits of my family and myself."

Replace it with: "I cook healthy meals more than I do bad ones. Life is about balance, and today that means that we order pizza."

Scenario: You went out on a date that did not meet your expectations and values.

Negative thought: "I will never find anyone on my level."

Replace it with: "Love will come to me, when it is right for me. I am open to receive it, and I am grateful for what is coming. In the meantime, I will focus on my personal growth, on being able to offer my true authentic self to the person who really deserves me."

> **Scenario:** You didn't get that business deal you hoped for.
> **Negative thought:** "I knew it wouldn't work out. I must not be good enough."
> **Replace it with:** "When one door closes another one opens. What is important is to push forward no matter what and in doing so new opportunities will come!"

You get the picture.

This is not a sprint. It's a long-distance effort and sometimes what feels like a grueling marathon. You need to take your time and practice—everywhere, and all the time. Imagine you are a runner training for a marathon. You won't see all the effects of your training in one day; however, gradually, over time, you will improve.

I'm saying it again... negative thoughts rob you of being present in your business, in your personal life, and as a parent. It's about what you decide. You have to feel fulfilled and emotionally satisfied at the office *and* at home. How do you operate a business that has lucrative scaling potential while living life on your terms? This is an essential question being asked today. *Replacing* the thoughts that don't serve you is the answer. Otherwise, you place limitations on your future success. But remember, you aren't doomed because you had one negative or fearful thought; however, you *are* doomed if you maintain this ineffective mental state. So, it behooves you to embrace the useful habit of replacing inefficient thoughts with ones that empower and propel you into a higher vibrational plane, where you will have better outcomes.

You are a vibrational being. Taking on this winning mindset is the first step in activating this higher vibrational energy state that will bring you even more wins. Period. This makes manifesting what you want to occur in your life (versus what you don't) the natural outcome... and only outcome. This is governed by the universal law we live in. Take, for example, golfers; they know this mental game far too well. Quite frankly, any successful athlete. A single-minded focus on their desire is a primary factor in achieving greatness.

Your Self Check-In

A big part of focusing on the outcome of your thoughts is to understand the influence that you have over your destiny. That is why it's important that you check in with yourself. Make it a habit. "How am I doing? How am I showing up for whatever the day might bring me?" You are your greatest asset. Everything you want—happiness, success, fulfillment—starts with how you show up for yourself first.

I have been in the sales industry my entire life. I know how important it is to maintain a positive mindset when interacting with people on a daily basis. Whether in sales or not, it is important. It's impossible to maintain an "Olympic 10" state of mind every single day! We weren't meant to. We are all human. Some days you feel a bit off; sometimes tired, feeling sick; sometimes frustrated, sad, or disappointed. Whatever it is, all human emotions are valid but not always warranted. It certainly doesn't lessen your value as a person.

These moments of weakness are opportunities for self-compassion. *Feel* what you feel; but don't allow it to corrupt your concentration, confidence, or your needed performance. In fact, when we're experiencing negative emotions like stress, anxiety, anger, etc., our judgment will be clouded or compromised, thus reducing our dynamic potential. Armed with this newfound awareness, you can become even more intentional about interrupting negative thought patterns and redirecting your focus and intent. By now you are aware that you can change your state in a matter of *seconds*—if you need to.

Check in with yourself. If you simply need to take a break and regroup—do so unapologetically. If you need a moment to breathe—do so. By cultivating conscious awareness of your current emotional state and how you present yourself to the world, and to loved ones, you're taking a significant step toward personal and interpersonal growth. Sometimes discussing your current emotional state with a loved one or a trusted friend can help you too. If I am feeling a bit off my game and in need of a private moment to reboot, instead of taking that needed moment, I snap at my children, get frustrated with my husband, or express impatience with my employees, then WHO wins?

But if I am feeling off balance and then tell my kids, *"Mommy is not feeling her best right now and needs a moment to herself (a time out). Can you please entertain each other for a bit?"* What is the lesson here? You are teaching your children: (1) self-care is important; (2) observing and being in tune with your behavior and needs are important; and (3) that everyone should take the time to make sure they are showing up better for themselves and those around them.

You are also subconsciously setting the right expectations for future interactions. This honest vulnerability of expression isn't reserved for relating with your children alone; you do the same with intimate as well as professional relationships. You can't give to others what you don't possess. Nourish your mind, body, and spirit, and everything else flows from there.

Here is a simple formula with examples to follow. It works wonders:

1. Express how you are feeling.
    (*"Hey, I am having a rough time"*)
2. Ask for what you need.
    (*"I need a minute to breathe"* or *"I need help with dinner"*)

For this magic to occur, you have to ask yourself—and be honest with yourself—"*How are you REALLY doing?*" As an inspirational speaker, I myself know when I am feeling a bit off. If I ignore my unresourceful state of mind, consequences occur, and my performance suffers. This means my audience suffers too. Your mood must be treated with the utmost importance, performance-wise. It determines your state of mind, and this determines how you show up based on how you *feel*.

And what follows? As we've discussed, it's what you attract. This is because your feelings create a vibrational energy that sends a corresponding frequency into the universe, which then draws similar circumstances to you. Understanding this is key to intentionally shaping your reality through preparation and observation. Remember, your greatest supporter in all endeavors should be yourself.

If you're waiting for the world to tell you, "Hey, slow down! You need a break to regroup and recharge," you'll never get to be the best you. Why? No one knows you like *you do*, no matter how close they are to you. No one else will be more in tune with you than *you*. Who, other than God, naturally cares about your needs? You! Sure, it is nice to be acknowledged by your peers and loved ones. But their approval shouldn't be your goal. Stop trying to prove that you're a good enough mom/parent, a good enough leader, a good enough partner; that you are capable enough; that you're attractive enough. You are enough as you are. Don't allow other people's unwanted negative seeds attempt to get planted in you. Reject it! You decide if you allow it or reject it. You shouldn't value yourself based on public opinion. Because you won't be able to show up as the best version of yourself. Instead, you will be living the dream of others, which will make you an internally hollow person. You are uniquely you in the most beautiful way. There is literally no other human out there like you. It is time to let your unique gifts shine. Like pop singer Rihanna sings, "Shine, bright like a diamond!"

When I was a single mother after my divorce, I was constantly hearing people around me say, "Oh, it's so hard to date, especially if you have kids and all that emotional baggage." Yes, I did have what society calls baggage. We all do. But guess what? It's MY beautiful baggage. It was created in my life by me, living as the best human I knew how to be. I truly believed that I would find a person who would appreciate my emotional scars as badges of honor for my personal growth, not as something to be ashamed of. I believed that this person would be fortunate to have me in their life—because I learned how to be my biggest fan. Your self-esteem should not be wrapped up in someone else's validation of you. Surrender the version of you that seeks approval from others.

Embracing my insecurities and my experiences, while still working on myself, is how I learned how to fall in love with myself. I was worthy of love. I knew that I was a great catch. This attitude was not coming from a place of conceit. I was being my authentic self, instead of pretending to be someone else in order to appease others. My two kids and I were worthy of something more. I was a dedicated mother, a driven professional with unbridled goals, overflowing with self-confidence, who still believed in the power of love. Being with a partner one day for the rest of my life was the added cherry to my already beautiful life.

I pray that you find something that strikes a chord within you to take action in your life, and in an area that desperately needs it. I challenge you to take an honest hard look at yourself at this moment. Now is as good a time as any. Nothing is more important than getting your life together. Whatever you make your top priority you will see it in your results every time, without fail. You need to look at yourself in the mirror; be willing to have that courageous, uncomfortable conversation, the one you've been putting off. If you cry, it's because you are finally facing the one person who you needed to face the most—you. Let the tears flow. Because who are you kidding anyway? You can kid your partner, your friends, and your social media followers... but you cannot kid yourself. You have to go within and do the work required. Face the pain that feels like shackles holding you back.

In asking yourself those tough, honest questions, start with...

- Are you the real you?
- Are you a watered-down version of the environment's expectations of you?
- Do you like yourself?
- Do you love yourself?
- Do you have fun hanging out with *you*?
- Do you feel valuable? To your relationships, to yourself? In your business?

These are questions you need to be able to answer before you can show up for others in your life. You need to love yourself—first. You need to love yourself unconditionally so that if you mess up, you aren't berating yourself with shame and criticism. Instead, shower yourself with compassion and grace. You must be to yourself what you want others to be to you.

How do you fall in love with yourself? Well, one way is to *be kind to yourself*. We have been taught since we were young that we need to be kind to others. But why hasn't anyone taught us how to be kind to ourselves? Embracing our imperfections is another path to self-love and kindness, for they are our most valuable assets. See them for what they are. Remember that self-love is the foundation for genuine connection with others. Be vulnerable with yourself. I promise you that doing this kind of self-care will allow you to feel the needed empathy whenever you encounter disappointment of any kind.

Ancient Greek philosopher Socrates famously originated the phrase *"Know Thyself!"* This insight buttresses the fact that knowing who you *truly* are—your *inner* strengths, flaws, values, and imperfections—all contribute to achieving your goals. You aren't just talking and planning your goals. You are doing the appropriate activity to make them a reality. When we truly understand who we are, we are better equipped to convert our goals from bland aspirations into concrete actions. Self-awareness is directly tied to your self-image, self-acceptance, and internal energy, all leading toward personal success.

So, do yourself a favor and make personal check-ins a habit. Self-reflect not only on yourself, but on your milestones and what else you choose to accomplish; check in on your grand plan and purpose as well. You can also be more present and supportive for yourself and for those around you, whether in business, socially, or personally. *Make things happen!* Your fuel tank will overflow with confidence when you do so.

You are never too old or too young to start on an amazing journey that is so rich with delight that it scares you. Ignite the beginning of your journey. Raise your standards of yourself and those around you.

How to Start?
- Write five things you love about yourself.
- Write five things you think people love about you.
- Write five things you can do today to improve how you feel now.
- Schedule a date with yourself on your calendar. Do something you love. Feed your soul!
- Schedule a regular check-in on your calendar. It can be daily, weekly, or monthly, depending on your needs.

Happiness Is Not Something You Seek

- Cultivate good mental health habits during the day. Simple actions, like a five-minute break for deep breathing, can work wonders in centering you or having a sense of calm in a hectic day, often more than you might realize.

It's crucial to be at peace within yourself, to feel self-love stirring within, so that you can be at your best for others—and for yourself. These suggested exercises will help you to get in touch with *YOU*. Your children, partner, and clients want you to show up for them in a way that makes them feel as if they are the most important person in the universe, building and increasing the trust bond between you and them. That is also how you gain their support and love—when you are being responsive and understanding of their needs in the moment.

"You make known to me the path of life; you will fill me with joy in your presence..."

—Psalm 16:11

CHAPTER 5

Sorry, Not Sorry

"Listen to the mustn'ts, child.
Listen to the don'ts.
Listen to the shouldn't, the impossibles, the won'ts.
Listen to the never haves,
then listen close to me...
Anything can happen, child.
Anything can be."

—Shel Silverstein

Ever since I was a child, I have had the mentality of a wild thing. A polarity responder, you might say. You tell me something can't or shouldn't be done; and I'll tell you, *"Watch me!"* Have you noticed that when kids are young, they possess this "anything is possible" attitude? That is until parents or society intervenes to "correct" their unrestrained optimism by killing or suppressing it. I have always loved this quote, because it's true: "The word '**Impossible**' consists of '*I'm Possible!*'" Everything is impossible until it's accomplished, so what stops YOU from being the person to make that impossible thing happen? If everyone had this impossible mindset, we would still be living as we did in the 1800s, or earlier! Someone, in just about everything you see around you, had a thought, had an idea, had an *"I'm possible idea."* They became the disrupter. So why not you?

Preserving that innocent childlike mindset is your birthright. This is how you were born. This is how God created you and me. When you understand that this is how you are meant to live your life, untainted by societal norms and expectations, then you'll discover these attitudes from childhood are an asset that can help build dreams later in life. If you think you've lost this childlike wonder, the good news is that it is still there. You can still access this state of mind with confidence—focusing your mind on what you want, your goal, being brave and relentless in your pursuit. Having a mindset that you'll do "whatever it takes." Unapologetic success in anything you are invested in has no chance but to occur.

In previous chapters we explored how the influence of others can significantly impact our thinking, both positively and negatively. In other words, the power of external perspectives can either inspire and uplift you, or lead you astray, diminishing your unique vision. External influences turned me into a people pleaser, always the *yes* person who allowed just about anything, because I lacked boundaries and filters. Fortunately, I eliminated those disastrous external influences from my life the moment I set boundaries and filters. This dictated the behaviors, attitudes, and standards I was willing to accept from others and what I expected of myself. Boundaries gave me the freedom to express who I truly am, and allowed me to accomplish what I wanted to, without the added external pressure.

Be Unapologetic for Your Ambitious Goals

If I received a penny for every time someone offered me their unsolicited opinion and belief, I'd be a billionaire twice over by now. These myopic opinions and beliefs, disguised as advice, were upsetting because they were designed, intentionally or otherwise, to constrict what I wanted to accomplish, trying to convince me that my audacious ambitions were impossible to attain. When I earlier told you that you should learn to love and honor your *true* authentic self, this also includes accepting and pursuing your dreams. Self-love and authentic acceptance also mean being comfortable when striving for whatever it is that your heart desires, relentlessly—*regardless* of external opinions and judgment. This will also come in handy when the sneaky surprise of life, as they say, deals you a bad card of circumstances. Forces, external and/or internal, will tempt you to give in, to give up. Here is *when you are required* to push through.

Sometimes You Have to Fight for Your Dreams

Take time for yourself to figure out your life's journey, doing the things that light your heart on fire. Because God does not plant these seeds of desire for nothing. They are there for a purpose. And when you're not listening to it, you start to feel unsatisfied. A bit frazzled. You may not even know why, but this is why. I'm telling you; I was there. I promise you that when you start doing the very thing that you feel the most aligned with, your true purpose, you love, your life will shift in a way that you never thought possible. When I finally landed a publishing deal, I shared the news with my older brother: "I feel like I'm dreaming." He responded, "You feel like you're dreaming because you're living your dream." His words almost made me cry. He was so right! I can't wait for you to experience this.

If you don't yet know what it is you love doing, get in a place of inner work. Silence. Meditate. Ask for guidance. Ask for clarity. Remember—ask for what you want. Yes, searching your soul is a form of asking for what you want. You will receive answers. Don't rush this self-discovery process. It is your beautiful journey, in God's beautiful time.

Your goals don't have to make sense to anyone—but YOU! You are the only person who decides how big you want to dream.

Furthermore, when growing up, parents, friends, neighbors, basically anyone in a perceived position of authority in a child's mind will exert influence of some kind. Case in point, our primary influencers—parents. They consciously and subconsciously teach us that there are certain approved or tried-and-true paths you must take in life (according to whom?). Our parents aren't bad or malicious in their intentions; their behavior springs from innate love and protection for us, just as their parents did for them. However, parental protection of a child can have the opposite effect, meaning it restrains dreams instead of liberating them. You then become the individual consumed by guilt, regret, and resentment, simply due to unfulfilled dreams. Imagine the person you can be and will become when you summon the courage to pursue what you felt in your heart was true for you.

In general, your loved ones want to protect you; this includes shielding you from what they *perceive* as failure. Projecting their fears onto you is one tactic they use to achieve this... until you believe them. Thus, you have succumbed to their will. Though well meaning, this protection also lays bare the fact that they don't believe in *your* goals as strongly as you do, because of *their* limiting belief. Face it, sometimes parents just can't comprehend the gravity of your willpower and abilities, and what you want, or I should say *need*, to accomplish. They just want to keep you safe for the sake of being safe.

Repeat after me:

"NOBODY HAS TO APPROVE MY DREAMS! THEY ARE MY DREAMS AND NO ONE ELSE'S."

You don't need permission to live your truth! You don't need to apologize for your ambitious goals, and you certainly don't need to feel guilty that you want to live life on your terms, and with real purpose.

Society has deceived us into believing that education and doing well in school, graduating high school, then on to college, and securing that coveted job is the *only* path to a fulfilled life. This final destination, the goal, masquerades as "success!" The fact that society has normalized this belief doesn't mean it is true… for every occasion. But God knows I am guilty of wanting to protect my children from the unknown as well.

I remember having a conversation with my oldest son when he told me he wanted to pursue a career in music instead of continuing his education at Long Island University in Brooklyn, New York. This was my son's passion; this was his dream. My son knew he wanted to do this, as much as he knew he needed to breathe. And knowing what I now know, I understood his drive. But I still had the innate urge to protect him, simply because I didn't think his musical path should have been his only option. I struggled to find arguments against his dream. My son chose his path. And here I was doubting it. *"Pursue your dreams; never let anyone tell you otherwise,"* is what I instilled in my son while raising him. Now, my mind was consumed with lists of "what ifs."

"STOP it, Mama Bear!" I told myself, after realizing what I was doing. Who the hell was I to tell my son not to pursue what sets his heart on fire? I taught him growing up to never settle for anything less than what made his heart smile, and to have the courage to pursue his dreams. I instilled in my son that there was no limit to what you could achieve.

I couldn't go back on what I always championed. I knew I had to let my son take his path and have him live his own dreams, and I would be there cheering him on, wherever that might lead. Part of our role as parents to protect our kids is to also protect their dreams.

The decisions we make can lead to success or growth. Even when you think it was the wrong choice, maybe it was the right one in that moment. Even if it doesn't work out, it's never failure. It comes with growth and pride that you pursued something most are afraid to do. If we don't pursue things because we are afraid of making a mistake, then we'll never see what awaits us on the other side. Which mindset do you think orients toward resilience? Every one of our decisions, even bad ones, is a part of growing, of maturing, of aiding in building your personal sense of identity and self. My job as a parent is to support that, not to prevent it. My job as a parent is to protect those dreams; not to file them under the label "impossible."

I admire my son's bravery for coming to me with his life's plan. My son didn't ask for my permission, he took charge; my young man had already made his mature decision. The only thing left was for him to receive my blessing, which I lovingly gave to him. I am eternally grateful that I found the strength in my heart to realize how important my role as a protector of his dream is. Because he did what most people are too afraid to do—pursue a career in music on his own terms, of his own free will, unapologetically following his dreams.

As a matter of fact, his bravery served as a catalyst and inspiration for my own growth, which I will reveal in the next chapter.

What is it that YOU dream about? What is your "*I'm Possible*"?

Do you want to …

- Travel the world?
- Go for that promotion?

- Go bigger in your business?
- Start a family?
- Start that business?
- Retire young?
- Find true fulfillment?

You can wear your blessings well and still contribute to the world. Our mission is bigger than ourselves. Even bigger than the number of houses we possess, or the number of "zeros" in our bank account(s), as long as you don't lose yourself in the process by placing a bigger meaning on the material riches you've been blessed with. This is what matters. You will lose—big time if your happiness is based on external sources and objects, versus the wealth that's already within.

You can win in life, be happy, and be fulfilled because you found your sense of purpose. True, we won't take our material possessions to Heaven, but if this is your desire now, why not go for it? You want to wear those Gucci shoes? Do it! If you desire a partner who's right for you, go for it! If you always dreamt of having your own business, START today! If you are ambitious in your mind, it is there for a reason, so why not go for it? God didn't create you so that you are destined to settle or live mediocre lives! He made you happy. He made us all with an abundance of capability to create any life we want. Our Creator wants you to go for it! A basket laden with the fruits of desire and dreams awaits you. You only need to seize this God-given basket Our Creator has made available for you. You won't starve when you align yourself with the fruits of desire. Because you are living life with purpose. It's how God intended us to live. I always say "wear your blessings well, unapologetically." It's not the material things we will take with us but the woman or man we became in the process of earning them!

The late nights; the sacrifices. The seasons we chose faith over fear! So yes, I wear my blessings proudly.

Living the way that God wants us to live also demands that we understand the power of personal values. They dictate what you say yay or nay to. We pursue what we value the most. Everyone has different values that take priority. You say, "I don't have time to go to the gym." But when it comes to caring for your nails or your hair that is a "must" on your list, right? (Am I right, or am I right?) The same goes for the goals we pursue and the things that become a MUST. If you are not uncomfortable with where you are, then how likely are you to change? You will change when your circumstances become a MUST.

Example: The way you eat is affecting your health negatively. *So, now, it becomes a must for you.* "I must do it now!"

Not everyone wants that expensively envious BMW, or that vacation home with a pool, or dreams of becoming a billionaire. Some people simply have more altruistic desires. Either of these is OK. Why? Because that is your desire, your goal, and your "WANT!"

Whatever it is that you want, ask yourself:

- What is the purpose behind my goals?
- What will this do for me?
- Who will I become?
- What will I be able to do, now that I achieved this?
- Who can I help on this journey?
- How can I contribute?

As we learned in the previous chapter, happiness is not a destination. So if you are using your goal to achieve so-called happiness, that is the wrong way to go about it. That doctorate degree won't make you happy. That Rolex glistening on your wrist won't make you happy. Chasing money won't make you happy. That self-discovery trip to Italy will only have you bring a couple of extra pounds home from all that delicious pasta you endured. But if you find fulfillment in what you want and a *true* purpose, then that is not about greed; it's about growth and personal happiness. That is why it is so important to wear your blessings well, show off your accomplishments with pride, and seek your dreams—unapologetically hard. True happiness resides within, so you have to uncover the true meaning behind what it is that your heart and soul want.

I've witnessed firsthand how some demonize material wealth, labeling money as the root of all evil. This belief, I find, is often held by those who struggle financially throughout their lives, creating a negative relationship with money, which hinders their abundance. Yet, I believe we're meant to experience life fully, and if that includes enjoying life's finer things, there's no need for you to apologize for working hard to afford them. Evil doesn't stem from wealth itself, but from a misguided and uneducated pursuit of it, believing money equates to happiness.

True fulfillment lies elsewhere. Money, however, is a valuable tool. It enables experiences, like the immense joy I felt as a single mom taking my entire family (including my sibling and his kids) to SeaWorld, creating lasting memories. My own financial aspirations—becoming a top producer in real estate—were rooted in a desire for security and the freedom to be present for and emotionally available to my children, something the traditional job didn't offer. Having a home in an affluent neighborhood of my choice also meant safety, a stark contrast to my childhood in rough areas, particularly our first San Diego apartment where, at nine, I feared the walk home from the bus stop. Or flying my mom first class because I want her to experience the finer things in life; something she's never had the pleasure of doing for herself.

There's no need to apologize for your desires.

When you see the progress that you are making in whatever it is that you are pursuing, you will feel a sense of fulfillment from that alone. It is not just about the target and your arrival; it's about the journey and what it is molding you to be. Who is the person you are growing into? What is the knowledge you're gaining that money can't buy?

Fall in love with the here and now. Fall in love with your sense of faith; fall in love with the imperfections of your goal, fall in love with adopting the mindset that you will discover more than you ever thought. If everything is in divine order, then circumstances, events, and experiences will all play out the way they were ordained to. The money will always follow. God will never allow a door to close that was meant for you. Our Creator *opens* doors—of opportunity. It was not meant for you if it closes. You are always being divinely guided, even when it hurts, and even if at the time you don't know *why* your current circumstance is occurring. Trust the process. Let go and let God do the work he is doing behind the scenes. Leave room to make God a part of your journey. A part of your team.

For example, do you want to have money so you can help your parents and eliminate the financial stress from their lives? Do you want to travel to learn from other cultures so you can share what you learned with the world in your book? Do you want to raise enough money so you can afford to make a real change in the world and start that nonprofit? Do you want to teach others how to make money, because you had nothing once upon a time, until you learned the secret to success?

Having things, material things doesn't equal fulfillment. Having a purpose does.

The Regret Factor

Picture this: You are on your deathbed, your fingers, wrinkled by the weight of your life-long toil, clutching pictures of the past. Your eyes begin to water; emotion feeds a lump in your throat, causing it to grow. Suddenly, you look up at your loved ones and say, "Gee, I wish I had done more of what people told me I should do."

Yeah, right!

According to a University of Scranton report, just 8% of individuals achieve their New Year's goals. We are talking New Year's goals and promises. Now imagine and extend this throughout the year, individuals (or groups) wanting to set and achieve a goal, or goals. Chances are these numbers are the same. Why is this? It's not about the time of year you set goals. Nonsense! It's the mindset and strategies required to Make Things Happen. Yes! To Make Things Happen!

The biggest thing to fear is living in regret. Many give up on their dreams and goals way too soon.

- "I don't have what it takes."
- "I don't have enough money."
- "I can't do what I love because I have kids."
- "I'm too busy to do that right now."

And on... and on. Sounds familiar?

This doesn't have to be you! That's why you are reading this book... because you want something more. You want to know that you can change your life. You can step into more, whatever more looks like for you. You can begin something greater than where you are now, at any age, any time, under any circumstances. Because I can tell you this, at the end of your life, you would care less about other people's opinions and their neatly boxed norms of what's acceptable and appropriate.

Did you live your dreams, and did you fulfill your purpose? I can promise you this: You living in alignment with your purpose will bring you happiness. It's about the action you take every day and asking yourself, am I living in alignment with my purpose? It's okay if you have an off day. What matters is that you get back on track. It is never too late. Age matters not! There's still time to do what makes you happy and fills your soul with joy. You just have to allow yourself to desire it with no psychological borders. Allow it the space to be bigger than anything else that you've ever wanted—create it!

Your potential and opportunities are full of possibilities. However, keep this in mind… the biggest restraints and setbacks are often influenced by our behavior and our fears. The action you take, or inaction, will always appear in the results you get. When you know this, it gives you the know-how to make a different choice.

Ask for What You Want

I can hear the non-believers in the back mumbling that you don't get *everything* you want. True! However, there is a reason for that.

Dwayne "The Rock" Johnson is an actor, entrepreneur, and a former wrestler. Dwayne had a dream. So during his youth he trained hard, devoting every moment toward it—to play at the Super Bowl with his team. Life happened, other opportunities presented themselves, and he took a completely different path. Dwayne is massively successful today, wealthy, and has a business acumen few performers possess.

Dwayne, still with that subtle twinkle of desire burning in the back of his mind, often speaks about his regret of abandoning his childhood dream. But did he really give up on his dream? From an alternate perspective it certainly looks that way—but he didn't. Instead, Dwayne refocused his efforts to explore the opportunities that presented themselves to him. He took full advantage of every situation, every contact, and every idea. He was relentless in creating an empire, surrounding himself with professionals and supporters, people who believed in him and his work. He is a skilled promoter who grew his business ventures exponentially, receiving awards and recognition.

And you know what else he did? He opened the Super Bowl LVI at SoFi Stadium on Sunday, February 13, 2022.

True, "The Rock" wasn't playing on the field. But he fulfilled his lifelong dream. He came full circle, as he often says, with everything that led him to this moment when he realized that being flexible with your destiny is imperative for fulfilling your purpose.

You might think you know better; you might think at that moment you want something other than what is being presented to you, but guess what? There might be something even better for you than you could have imagined!

There might be a path that you haven't even considered that will prepare you for something even bigger than anything you could have imagined! So when things don't immediately happen, don't despair and give up. Fight for your dreams. Fight to grow and fulfill your destiny, not for what society dictates you should want! (Should want? According to whom?)

There's no need to copy someone else's dream. Be your unapologetic, authentic self, bringing to the world the miracle of YOU! Hold no space apologizing for who you are; hold no space for regretting who you might have been in your life! When you physically leave this earth, the people who you worried about pleasing, or those who created so much anxiety in your life, likely won't be around to attend your funeral.

I was completely obsessed with selling real estate in 2008. This was during the real estate bust. I worked my ass off, even pulling all-nighters; coffee was my best friend back then. Thinking that I was improving myself, I also insanely critiqued and picked at everything I did. It felt as if I had placed myself under a self-inspecting microscope. The truth is, my deeply held insecurities were in control, driving all my behaviors. This obsession with "perfection" drove me to the point of borderline madness. I wasn't there yet, but I was certainly heading in that direction.

Having self-compassion and self-empathy are key ingredients needed for personal success. Those I forgot. Or, to be honest, I chose to ignore. If you are incessantly too hard on yourself and callously pushing and pulling, it will backfire—on you. You need to find it in your heart to balance your work, life, skills, and abilities. A master-archer knows not to pull on the bowstring for a prolonged time. Constantly doing so weakens the bowstring's potency and explosive potential, rendering the entire instrument useless, and technically lifeless!

To *"Keep It Simple and Succulent"* (k.i.s.a.s.) just aim and shoot, knowing within your spirit of resiliency that everything will work out. There's no need to overthink it. The biggest regret you can have is the shot you didn't take, the opportunities you didn't pursue, the ideas you didn't create; the people you didn't let in.

Begin... even if it looks messy.

Living without regrets takes being present in every moment, and being open to what's next, and most important... being kind to yourself and to the people around you, for they are your support system. An opportunity sometimes knocks once. Will you take it?

Will you take that leap of faith? You may believe that you aren't ready yet. But remember, just like the master-archer, it simply takes practice to perfect your skill... and a love for yourself.

Let Your Dreams Take Flight

Remember when I said how obsessed I was with my real estate career to the point of madness? Clutching so tightly on to something makes you lose sight of who you are and especially of who you want to be. You have to provide the space for your dreams to grow and flourish. You have to give it the sunlight of attention, the water of love, and you have to raise them tenderly as you would a delicate plant. But let me be clear: The fact that you are carefully crafting your life's mission and purpose doesn't mean that your ideas should lack the boldness of an entrepreneur and the daring attitude of a skydiver. On the contrary!

In pretty much every company I have collaborated with, I utilized a "dream catching" exercise, as I call it. This is the creation of a vision board. I can tell you absolutely wild stories about the power of focusing your mind on the tangible goals you are seeking. For some of the companies I worked with the results we brought in were astounding. I want to share my story of my first vision board and how it changed my life.

Things were changing so fast for me; I was excited! I remember I was watching a TV program about the use of vision boards as a tool for manifestation. So I gave it a go. I was not even looking for anyone romantically at the time. In fact, I was avoiding it. But I knew deep inside that I would eventually remarry and that special someone to share the rest of my life with was out there. I knew that I had to prioritize: First, raise my standards to what I truly wanted, which was not just any partner. I had to get clear on what exactly I wanted. I remember doing this exercise and I wrote down all the things I wanted in a life partner. The list was long! At the top of the list he had to like kids (hello, I had two) and he had to love his mom because I adore mine. So I created a vision board that outlined the main desires I had as far as that person goes, as well as my future with him.

What else was on my vision board? A lot! A picture of the dress I loved that I found in a magazine at my nail salon, that one day I would wear on my wedding day, and a picture of the ring I liked. I practically filled in the blanks on everything regarding the specific person—what they liked, what their values were and otherwise, what activities we'll do together, etc.

I honestly forgot about my vision board after I put it away. Then a year later, I met my husband. I later found my vision board. I was stunned at how accurate everything was! He liked exactly the same things I wished for, down to the crazy wish that my future husband had to also love snowboarding. (Boy did I regret that! The man wants to snowboard even at −3 degrees.)

I was speechless, stunned, floored!

Was this a magical board? No! It was simply me creating a very clear and compelling vision of what it looked like.

This simple testimonial demonstrating the subconscious mind's power further inspired me to continue. I was already dreaming of sharing the vast knowledge I had learned about the mind with the world. I was already dreaming of inspiring other people to achieve their goals, empowering them to find the treasure in themselves, and thus change their lives. At that point, though, I knew with all my being that my dream would become a reality. And guess what? Here we are today, with you holding the fruit of that dream in your hands.

Yes, of course, the journey to share my knowledge with the world has had its ups and downs, and lefts and rights. I put my dreams on hold for a time to work with my husband at the family company. I created plans for transforming companies around the globe with my results-driven sales training program. Then he asked me if I would start with his company. Why? He was inspired by my idea of my sales training I wanted to pitch to CEOs around the world.

I hesitated. I wanted to pursue *my* dream, and I knew this would slow me down. It took us three months to think about it and decide whether working together was a good idea. One, I had been my own boss for more than a decade. Was I now going to work for my husband? And two, would he even be able to afford me? Yes, I thought about that! "I'll give you a year," I said. Excited at the opportunity to embark on something new, I honored my promise to him. One year turned into two; two turned into three, until almost a decade. The company's growth was next level! We had fostered a completely new core value-infused culture that developed the company team to think bigger about how they make things happen. This more than quadrupled the company's size. This success further proved to me the power of how we make things happen really has. I needed to make my mission a priority. Fulfill my dream.

Let's not kid ourselves. Working and helping to grow the family business had its trials and tribulations. Every hardship builds our resilience, tests our faith, and even our capacity to keep going. Every obstacle we face makes us stronger. Every challenge teaches us lessons. Having said this though, the most important thing is refusing to wallow in your circumstances. I remember times having all this resentment toward my husband at his family business. I thought he took me away from my dream. But the truth and reality is that no one was keeping me there but me; the more time spent in the business, the more attached to it I became. He supported my dreams even if it meant taking a step back from the business or leaving it altogether one day.

I'm familiar with the business of communication as I grew up interpreting for my parents; in fact, Spanish was my first language. The business of helping people bridge the gap in communication felt comfortable and second nature to me. The difference we were making was bar none. Furthermore, I had cultivated a *make things happen* mindset in our business, which infused in me a sense of responsibility to keep this business culture mindset ongoing. This I was most proud of. In the end it was my decision that brought me to where I was.

And in parallel, it was my burning desire and passion that was going to get me where I wanted to be. My heart was still afire, and I knew that my journey was preparing me for something bigger and better. My husband? He was always supportive, since day one, of my dreams and what I wanted to achieve. This was the person he met, the person he fell in love with, the one who wanted to help change the world, knowing that others must have the same or similar pain I (and even my struggling parents) once had, yearning for more, but didn't know how to attain it.

It was time.

But even with all that transpires, we still sometimes need a catalyst, a little nudge that rolls the snowball of our dreams, turning them into an avalanche.

For me, that push was my oldest son's words. I remember them like it was yesterday.

"I am tired of seeing you inspiring so many other people, including me, inspiring me to pursue my dreams; yet, you are not following your dreams yourself. What are you waiting for? When you are 60?"

My son was right. I had put my dreams on hold. I fell into the comfortable rut of not going after what I wanted, because it was "not the right time." I knew I would do it "eventually" but was constantly waiting for the right time. And guess what? There will never be a right time to disrupt the status quo and go big on what you are after. If you are waiting for the perfect conditions to pursue what you want, you will simply never get it. This is exactly how you suffocate your dreams, with the notion that there are possible things and impossible things, that there are right and wrong circumstances/times, and that you are ready/not ready for it yet.

Don't suffocate your dreams.

My son lit the match and threw it in the pile of dry leaves. Feeling the heat of truth, of reality was what I needed. He was an ally in many ways.

Remember what I told you before? If your dreams don't scare you, then they are not big enough! Regardless of how scared you are, regardless of your fear of the unknown, or fear of failure, regret is much, much worse. Knowing that you tried, even if you didn't reach your destination, this is all you need to keep you whole. And avoid the heavy price of regret.

Think back to The Rock's story. Sometimes the goal you are going for might be unsuccessful at first. Life might surprise you by taking you in a new direction. Here's the thing though: This new path might be even more grandiose than anything you could have imagined. Who knows, in the end, you might even get what you wanted in the first place, albeit in a different form, just like The Rock did. That is why planting those seeds of desire, exuding that energy, attracting the right thoughts, circumstances, and people, and knocking on those doors currently closed, will ultimately lead you to where you are supposed to be. There's no need to doubt what I just said.

Have you encountered any successful people who experienced a completely effortless journey to the top? I haven't. The stories of success that you hear are stories of struggle, of being vulnerable and fearful. These stories are also about being strong and fearless, overcoming, persevering, struggling, and fighting for the end result, the prize just within eyesight. You have to fight the mythical dragon in the tower to save the princess. You have to walk into the mythological castle to throw the ring in and restore balance in the world. You have to invent 2,000 ways to create a light bulb. It's just the reality of it. And that's OK.

I know what it feels like to invest time and energy into something only for it to not take flight. It is hard—emotionally, too.

But our dreams won't manifest if we are inflexible. Sometimes that desired "yes" will appear in disguise, surprising you. It might resemble something completely alien to you. At times you might think you may have failed when, in fact, you succeeded! Following your dreams is never wrong. Just put in your best effort to let them roam free. Don't suffocate them over-thinking (aka analysis paralysis) and unwarranted caution.

It's okay to be feel frustrated. It's okay to feel impatient at times. What's *not* okay is to wallow in that mindset. The obsession that I had with real estate? Yes, desperate necessity brought it on, because I needed to pay my bills. Strangely though, that state of desperation forced me to excel, though in an unhealthy manner. I was pushing myself way too hard—and the wrong way, focusing entirely on the irrelevant, nano-like details right in front of me so much that I was missing the big picture, where success truly resided. What was the bigger picture? That an overstressed, frustrated, and exhausted mom is *not* what my kids deserve; that putting pressure on myself to succeed, at all costs, was consuming my life force, when, instead, less effort yielded greater results.

It was all about the energy you are putting out; think energy investment. Just like a boomerang, when you put your best effort in, you get the best results back. The energy I expended at that time in my life was one of fear, exhaustion, and stress. Of course, I would get that back. But once I realized that this was what I was doing to myself, I focused on how I framed my thoughts and what language patterns I was using with myself—self-talk is just a part of it!

Not only did I focus on what I was putting out, per se, but also on what I was sending into the public consciousness. Outside influences, the environment, and the people around me are all connected. This simply means they can either raise you up or push you down. That is the time when I refocused my obsession to understanding how the human mind and subconscious work for or against us, depending on what we were feeding it.

I began practicing "changing the channel" when a negative thought or influence was unfolding, and I allowed myself to stop stifling my dreams and let them roam free.

I never looked back, and I never apologized for who I am and how big I dream ever again.

"With man this is impossible, but with God all things are possible."
—Matthew 19:26

CHAPTER 6

Change the Channel

Struggles and adversity shape our character and build inner strength. This I know you know. Sure, you might call it a cliché. But guess what? It's true! Your biggest strength—the power of your subconscious—resides on the other side of struggle and fear. On the other side of hesitation even. I've mentioned time and again throughout this book how adversity has shaped successful people, how they defeat the obstacles and reap massive benefits from it.

Of course, the term *successful person* is a loose definition used to describe those you admire for their accomplishments, in any area. A successful person can be a billionaire; they can also be a stay-at-home mom. Whatever it is that you desire, whatever challenges you need to overcome, there's someone who has probably already done that. You have to learn to embrace what comes next and prepare the stage for your success. You are not just a sum of your basic traits, such as intelligence and talent.

You are an empowered person, possessing an unstoppable spirit! You become the commander of your fate when you learn to unleash it. God gave us all the power to create a beautiful life. You have free will. To jump as high as you wish, to reach the biggest goal you desire. Fate ultimately is in your hands by the decisions you actively make daily!

Embrace Change When It Knocks

When change occurs, it might seem as if everything is happening—all at once. But in reality, are they occurring because we attract them with our thoughts? Or are they happening because we finally have opened our minds to welcome what's possible?

Change may not always feel easy. As a matter of fact, more often than not, it can feel quite painful, no matter how much we say we are willing to embrace it. How much we believe we have a mindset that welcomes change, certain circumstances can challenge that notion, case in point, experiencing a painful transition, or simply perceiving ourselves as "not ready" for change. Think about it—when are you truly ready for a change? When is the right time? Change and challenges oftentimes go hand in hand. To buttress my point, I am not sure anyone would ever feel *ready* to lose a loved one, lose their job, or lose an opportunity. And yet, these events can and will be the catalyst for change that will lead to a key transformation in your life. How many times have you heard people say, "I'm not ready to have a baby?" then ... surprise! Change occurred. Yet, they adapted to it. Surprise! (Or no surprise.) Change is the one unavoidable, inevitable constant in our lives.

Yes, change can come to the rescue on a white steed, clutching a bouquet of roses in its mouth, exuding the aroma of opportunity. Likewise, change catalysts can indeed be circumstances that are less favorable. So, how do we deal with those situations? How do we push forward, especially when we feel at that moment that this is the most challenging time in our lives? Even though the principle you should follow is quite simple, pushing through can seem impossible. To be clear, I'm not saying it's always easy. But here is the biggest opportunity to pay attention to, the stories you tell yourself. For example, if you believe that this change will bankrupt you, it more than likely will. If you believe that you are not ready yet, you most certainly will not be. If you believe that loss will crush you, and you won't be able to recover, that is exactly what will occur. Take note: People always follow through on who they *believe* they are, or are not.

In the previous chapter, I talked about my complete change in career. I was a successful action-driven mindset coach and trainer. I felt fulfilled. Business was successful.

When I put my successful career on hold to devote my time to the growth of my husband's company, I used my knowledge and experience to build a sales team—from the ground up. I was up for the challenge of making things happen. And it intrigued me. I had incredible breakthrough moments during my journey there. We proved to be a highly formidable and successful husband and wife team. We each contributed our unique strengths, which made us a dynamo of a team. However, let's not kid ourselves; there is no denying the rollercoaster ride I was on for years. Working with your significant other has its set of challenges.

Remember, I was hesitant at first. I was in a good place mentally, with a successful career. The last thing I needed was to constantly prove to anyone that my intellect and competence were the sole reasons my husband chose me to build his sales team, and not because I am his wife. I was the best choice for the job. Period! Yet, the seed of opportunity to change entered my mind; it started taking root. It was not a change I took lightly; it wasn't one I was looking for either. But it was growing in me, confronting me with a choice—to embrace it or to keep fighting it.

I won't lie. I did fight the urge for a bit. I am sure that no matter what circumstances you are facing, you will go through that as well. And that is perfectly fine. It is natural, as weird as that sounds. But I will tell you this—when something is placed in front of you, there is a reason for that. Maybe it's about risks worth taking or building resilience. Perhaps it's even about unlocking your true self, letting your brilliance shine. The possibilities are endless. Or maybe it's simply about becoming the person ready to embrace your next great adventure. Who can say, but you—via experiential discovery.

Change is inevitable. Sometimes it's a welcome guest; other times, it demands a pivot, as we all experienced in 2020. Did you fight it, or did you embrace or adapt to it? Did you focus on how that experience will expand your capacity for growth, or did you reject it with every fiber of your being? Some people took the opportunity to spend more time with their kids, work on projects around the house, build on their skills, and start the business that they always wanted to. Others didn't do so well. How did YOU embrace it as a challenge? What did you learn from it? Did you discover the lessons it was holding for you? Or did you push against it with all your might? Which one do you think was more productive? You don't have to be a rocket scientist to understand that swimming against the current will not get you very far.

When you are facing challenges, I want you to think about this—*What is the alternative to this situation? What is this circumstance teaching me? What direction is it pushing me toward? Can it be worse?* Oftentimes, we make it a bigger issue than it has to be. Nothing in your surroundings will change ... until you change. Let's face it, oftentimes this change is forced upon us. Sometimes you might be given a chance to voluntarily change. But if you haven't yet learned the lessons that you needed to, then that change will be forced on you, to do exactly that behavior, until it becomes a *must* for you, out of desperation. Like your doctor sharing your lab work and saying you must improve your lifestyle, improve your eating habits, and start working on this, where it is no longer a choice.

The attitude that you use to filter your challenges through makes a bigger impact than you may think. It matters! If you sense it's going to be hard, it will be. If you change the way you see challenges, the challenges in your life will change ... in your favor! Again, I stress that it's all about your point of view. Your perspective. Two women I know lost their husbands in their 60s. Both grieved, of course; this is part of the process. However, one of them invested her efforts into being successful and productive on her own, while the other one did not feel capable.

One reframed her experience to become comfortable with being on her own and integrating the accompanying lessons she learned along the way. She had phenomenal progress in deliberately focusing on learning how to become her own person, after so many years of being part of a loving, supportive, and nurturing marital nucleus. It was hard at first. Naturally. But she persevered ... and succeeded. In her 60s, she began a new career, took part in a number of new activities she hadn't tried before, and focused on her remaining family. This new embrace of life helped her healing process and her self-growth. Her confidence strengthened.

In contrast, the other widow gave up, allowing grief to take full control. With every fiber of her being, this woman fought her new reality of having to live on her own. She focused on her grief so much that it became her *identity*. She nestled into that position without putting any effort of leaving it. She is lonely; she feels unfulfilled and believes her life is over. She even developed the ability to become spontaneously sick. Don't mistake grief as being a bad thing. Not at all. Grief is natural, and we all experience it. Everyone deals differently with this unavoidable emotion, and that's okay. We must find a way to move on from allowing the pain to cripple us. Not because we stop caring, or we stop hurting, because I don't believe we ever do. But because the person we lost would not want us suffering. Every challenge we face in our lives has a purpose when we live through it, regardless of what those circumstances are. What is not okay is to stay there and to allow that circumstance to become your identity. Take note:

- Your loss is not your identity.
- The mistakes you made in the past are *not* your identity.
- Being in an abusive relationship is *not* your identity.
- Struggling to make ends meet is *not* your identity.
- Procrastination is *not* your identity.

Get the point?

You have to build your identity and the meaning you're giving your circumstances. To do so, you must embrace the challenges that may come. Most importantly, be mindful of the stories you continue accepting by the personal language you tell yourself. By 'language' I also mean the images you build in your mind. Because, as you now know, you are creating your reality when you do this. If you believe it's going to be hard, it will be. Don't use the word try. Instead of I'll "try" to do this. Say I'll do my best to get it done. Notice the difference?

Imagine trying to "change the channel" of your thoughts. Instead of intentionally choosing a new program, you're just endlessly flicking through the options, never satisfied, never stopping. You'll scroll past potentially helpful channels without even noticing them—missing opportunities. Just like on TV, your thoughts dictate your emotional state. A comedy channel brings joy; a suspense channel brings tension and anxiety; and a horror channel brings fear. With challenges, it's the same: your perception, the channel you tune into, shapes your experience and your outcome. Remember, the angle at which you perceive *challenges* matters.

I cannot stress this enough—yes, there may be hard things you are facing, but how you perceive those moments will likely determine how you feel about them. Consequently, that feeling will influence the energy you expend into the universe; yes, the universe that never stops working *for* you, based on the intentional rhythm of your energetic drum.

The Power of Your Words

Practice with purpose to get this mindset pitch perfect. This includes me as well. I had five-hours' worth of work but only two hours to get it done while my nanny was there taking care of my babies.

"No way I can get it done in two hours," I told myself. But then I caught myself and said, "Hold on, Diana. This will not empower you! This will not bring you to the other side victorious! It matters how you feel in order for you to beat the odds."

Having the right perspective can do wonders. I changed my inner dialog, my mental attitude, and I asked myself the question: "*I wonder how much I can accomplish in the next two hours?*" Do you notice the difference? How we speak to ourselves and what questions we ask ourselves in those circumstances is of great importance. If nothing else, come from a place of curiosity. Even this small shift will produce better answers. This is just a small example—now imagine applying it to the bigger things in your life. Where else could you start changing the questions you ask yourself?

It is so much more empowering when the challenge leaves the opportunity for you to reach your potential instead of limiting it with the veil of impossibility.

My youngest son was about to lose his first tooth, and he was so excited. He waited such a long time for this. We were just as excited for him, too. Long story short, my son lost this tooth during school. Of course, the school nurse was kind and gave him a little box to keep his tooth, so he wouldn't lose it. It was a big deal.

On the way home from school in the car, just three minutes from home, he excitedly showed me his loose tooth. Then, it slipped from his grasp and vanished somewhere between his legs, getting lost in the car seat's crevice. A frantic search for the tooth proved hopeless.

At that point, we were already home. My little one was crying; I told my husband what happened. He turned to our son and said, "Buddy, I am sorry to break it to you. There is a good chance we won't find it." My son promptly starts whaling louder, now snot and tears are streaming down his face, as a look of disbelief and anger washed over mine. If you could kill with a glance, this is what I was guilty of.

"Why would you say that?" I reacted immediately. "Why would you build an image of failure for the future?" (You may think I'm being overdramatic, but this way of thinking translates into bigger areas in our lives.) You don't have to over-promise. But you have to have *hope* that it's possible. When you have hope, then everything changes. *Hope gives you vision, it's the spark that says, "maybe things can be different."* "We will do our best to find it!" There was no doubt in my voice when I spoke.

And guess what? We did! Now, I am not saying that each and every time something goes wrong, that we utter *words of possibility* and it's a guaranteed win. Of course not. However, you will clearly, without a doubt, increase your chances that things will work in your favor. This is vibrating with intention. Remember the universe will fulfill your desires or the feeling of lack/fear based on the *intentional* rhythm of your energetic drum. If you are bringing into your life a vibration of hopelessness, discouragement, and failure, *that is what you will attract! If it is of possibility? Then that is what you will also attract!*

A study titled "The Impact of Hope and Resilience on Multiple Factors in Neurosurgical Patients" (Duggal et al., 2016) focused on the impact of stable psychological characteristics on the emotional and functional recovery of patients. The study showed that the patient's mental state, especially during times of emotional distress, contributes to their recovery outcome. The study also concluded that *hope* acts as a protective factor in those circumstances. Some of these circumstances include patients facing life-threatening issues. It sounds so simple, and yet very few people realize the impact those factors have.

It is a no-brainer, right? Well, for self-aware individuals it is a no-brainer. Even researchers emphasize that acknowledging the link between mindset and outcome can improve a patient's chances. It's a testament to the incredible power of the human mind. Your mental state can signal to your brain to block pain and accelerate healing. No wonder researchers deem it as the single most important feeling state, the feeling of hope.

As my teacher, renowned co-founder of Neurolinguistic Programming (NLP), Dr. Richard Bandler once told me: *"When you change how you think, it will change how you feel, and in turn, it will change what you are capable of."*

A story I'll share is one very personal to me and also where miracles prove to be possible. One that confirms not only the power of your words but also the faith you put in what you say.

There was a period of my life when I struggled with anemia. For years doctors could not figure out what the issue was. Once finally diagnosed, medication was prescribed to support my body's production of healthy red blood cells, and I took the medication as directed. I asked the doctor how long I would need to be on this medication? Until the foreseeable future, he said.

Those who know me know I challenge traditional medicine. Don't get me wrong, I know medicine has helped many people, and I see the value in many instances, including myself. However,

I also believe in trying other methods *first*, more holistic options to see *what else is possible*. I use traditional medicine as more of a plan B.

Not satisfied with that answer, I went to multiple doctors, the best I could find. Finding myself in New York I asked the doctor *when* I get to normal levels with my red blood cells, will I be able to stop the medication? The doctor said something that truly threw me off my rocker. She said, "You will never likely get to normal levels." I was floored; no, livid! I left there with my husband on our two-hour trip home so upset. "How dare she tell me that? How does she know!? I'll be damned if she is going to tell me what my destiny regarding this is. I'm going to get to my normal levels. Watch!"

My husband unsuccessfully tried calming me down. I remember crying, dropping to my knees, even asking God what was I supposed to do? I knew I had to surrender it to God. That is exactly what I did. I was determined. I kept telling my doctors in Connecticut that I would get to normal levels.

Want to know the language I was saying? I believe that God is my pharmacy. I kept saying this over and over and over again. I remember asking the doctor in Connecticut if he had felt that I would be at normal levels, and he said he wasn't quite sure. And I asked him, "Doctor, do you believe in God?" He answered, yes. And I said, "Well, Doctor, with all due respect, He knows, and He is already taking care of this for me. You'll see." I kid you not he looked at me as if I had three heads. But deep down, I knew the doctor also had a look on his face as if my conviction persuaded him.

It was this undeniable faith I had and the power I gave the words I was speaking. About three months later, I got my labs back. And it came back showing I was at normal levels, and after years of anemia, I was no longer anemic. I cried and hugged my doctor, almost making him fall over. I was so overjoyed with this overwhelming feeling, where God said, why did you ever doubt me for even an ounce of doubt? I said, never again.

Whatever your worry, whatever your doubt, you can get through it a winner. I did not accept defeat to be my reality. Pay attention to the words you speak to yourself and even what others might say to you. Do they move you forward? Or do they create anxiety or doubt? Words matter. They manifest into our beliefs, and in turn determine how we react and choose to live our lives. When we accept as truth what others tell us we in essence, are being guided by their beliefs. Worst of all decisions are being made based on that. The doctor I saw in New York (the best of the best) had her own limiting beliefs about it. Does that make her a bad doctor? No, not at all. However, I do feel there is a level of ignorance that takes place in all of our professions where people are driven based on their own unique understanding; and in turn pass that on to others, by default.

Medical school doesn't teach you about miracles. The point is that I did not allow another human's limiting belief (even if they are the best doctor in town) to dictate my outcome. Call me delusional. Call me ignorant. I'll take it. Because I know to get what you want, sometimes you have to be willing to be a little radical and challenge others and their beliefs if that is what it takes, for you to end up with the outcome for your greater good.

Even in business I have seen this time and time again. People are so governed by their past experiences to dictate their future outcome. When I was in real estate in Connecticut, I had to work with attorneys for the first time during a closing. And the number of arguments I got into with some of them because I challenged their belief that it could not get done in a certain timeframe was so exhausting, to have to fight every battle for the sake of my clients getting the results they wanted. And it was not only in real estate. In many areas of business, I helped so many people get what they wanted because I was not afraid to ask and challenge a new way of thinking to empower change.

And guess what?

Why not you? The more you challenge this way of thinking, the more you'll see what's possible. Does it mean it will happen 100% of the time? Maybe not. But hear me; You'll get more of what you want by believing it's possible and challenging the status quo. If you live with this notion that "things can be different unless proven otherwise" you will be a winner. You are capable of anything your heart desires! Your God-given potential is there and ready to go. It only needs you to start the engine and put your foot to the pedal and go.

People who refuse to allow negative language, thoughts and images to saturate their mind during significant moments in time are just simply light years ahead of those who do. They don't allow that to take flight. They challenge it. Sometimes with all their might. This will undoubtedly increase your chances of a better outcome. Yes, sometimes it won't. But more times than not, I promise you, it will. See yourself a winner and you will become one.

Maintaining a "clean" mind offers a wealth of benefits. Your mind is often driven by the language you choose to utilize. It supports physical well-being, enhances academic success, fosters deeper connections, and strengthens your resistance to illness and outside influences. It cultivates a stronger sense of meaning, providing the grit and determination to overcome obstacles and reach your desired outcomes. The advantages are undeniable. Guess what, here's the best part: You get to choose the language you feed your mind, anytime, anywhere. You and only you get to decide whether you're going to entertain a negative thought driven by your language to take control of your mind. The only reason you feel afraid or anxious is because of a residual thought you are keeping alive. You can easily choose a different path, a different thought, even by saying, "What else can this mean?"

Language directionalizes the brain. The question is which direction does the language you speak move you towards or away? Below I am including some affirmations that move you forward. Affirmations "prime" the RAS (Reticular acitving system). For example, if you affirm, *"I attract opportunities for success,"* your brain starts noticing opportunities you may have previously overlooked. Be pro-active! Recite these! Add to them if you like! Get creative! I can write a thousand affirmations; we don't have enough pages here though. Affirmations work! Just as prayer does. Make it part of your daily habit to read them.

I am loved. I am worthy. I am safe.
I am deserving of all good things.
Everything happens for my greater good.
Anything that is meant for me will come and I am open to receive.
Today will be a great day!
I have the best love in my life.
I have an abundance of _(fill in the blank)_ flowing to me daily.
My faith is bigger than any doubts.
I am courageous.
Every day I get stronger.
Every day I release what does not serve me and I allow what does to enter my life.
All good things come my way.

It's Never a Failure

Our world is so unforgiving about "failure" that the very word feels tainted, sounds profane. What is failure anyway? You are unmarried at 30? You have no kids, and you are 40? You haven't graduated college? You've changed five jobs in the past year?

What makes someone say, "I have failed"?

Maybe it's the fact that if you don't achieve what society deems worthy, then you have *failed*. Sometimes it's as simple as selecting the wrong answer, or making the wrong decision, but isn't this what life is about? Nobody taught us how to "do life." We will always experience circumstances that challenge us, forcing us to make first-time decisions and risk making the wrong moves. Isn't that what living is all about, learning how to grow, learning from your mistakes, and experiencing life's crucial moments that move you forward, even if it looks like it has slowed you down—just temporarily?

The word failure is not even in my vocabulary. However, to clarify, we truly *fail* only when we quit; when we give into mind distractions and setbacks disguised as excuses. I reject the idea that living life and making decisions or choices can bring you to failure. It's never a failure! It's a lesson! It's an experience, *a moment of clarity and a moment of growth*. This only occurs when you encounter adversity. Can you imagine if EVERYTHING that you did went your way? Everything you pursued was a total success, 100% of the time? Who would you be right now? Adversity sculpts you into the person you are meant to be.

Maybe you left a secure job behind for something uncertain … You started a business that didn't go as planned. Or entered into a relationship that didn't work out … So what? These are all part of the human experience, and experiences are what make us who we are.

This, to me, is what life is *also* all about.

Whenever I interview a prospective employee, I always want to know if they've failed at anything and the lessons learned. Their response, their story will tell me all I need to know if they'll make a great candidate. While most employers might see failure as a weakness, this excited me. Because when you have someone on your team who has endured adversity, keep them. They've proven that they can weather the storm—with resilience and grit.

Release the notion that your life has to be perfect in the world's eyes!

Challenges are clues, something you need to learn. To stop, give up, refusing to go again is my definition of failure. When you pivot, when you struggle, when you fall, you always have to remember that there is something better on the other side.

God will not close doors that are meant for you. When it doesn't work out in your favor, it does not mean you've reached a dead end. It simply means God has something greater planned for you; Our Creator is forever working behind the scenes. We assume the worst when things don't work out. When something does not go right, I always remind myself that everything is happening *for* me, not to me. Rejection is nothing short of God's protection. When you walk through life, believing everything is happening for my greater good (even when it is so hard to swallow). It is almost a ritual chant to me now, an incantation repeat. Feel free to do so, too:

> *"Everything is happening for my greater good.*
> *So when things do not go as planned,*
> *or a door shuts,*
> *we have to be willing to pick ourselves up,*
> *to be our own cheerleader,*
> *and make room to what can come next.*
> *Be open to the possibilities that exist*
> *to shape who we want to be...."*

The only thing you have to ask yourself is, who do I want to be on the other side?

A Shortcut to Bravery

It may seem difficult to *"pull yourself up by the bootstraps"* when you are in the thick of the storm. I know. I've been there; I've struggled countless times. That is why I am here today to tell you it doesn't have to be that way. It doesn't have to be hard, long, and painful. You have the one thing that is readily available to you, the greatest gift that God gave us that you can access at any moment at any time of your choosing ...

Change the Channel.

Imagine that your brain is the most amazing TV screen in the world (which it is). This mental screen has the ability to show you ANY movie, any image you want to see, and even experience it as if it's happening in real time. Imagine sitting in a movie theatre only this time, you have the remote in your hands. Like a genie this screen responds to your wishes and commands.

Now picture that you are playing with your child or a friend, experiencing the feelings of laughter and joy, rainbows and butterflies. It's as if you are literally there in real time. Suddenly, a tornado swoops in, trashing everything! Debris strewn everywhere; dark, ominous clouds envelope the sky; the feeling of the high winds takes your breath away. Your heart races, your head pounds, and you simply can't look away. You know the tornado is behind the screen, that it can't hurt you, but seeing it that vividly, that close, rattles you to your core.

This is what negative thoughts do to you.

This is how you allow them to invade and take up residence in your mind, forcing their stay.

But wait! You have all the tools at your disposal to make that go away. You have the power of your conscious and subconscious mind, acting as combined tools—your remote to that TV screen in your brain. You can simply stop, take a breath, and choose to ... change the channel!

YOU can do that; nobody else can do it for you. Nothing will change unless you change the channel that you're on.

You have to *choose* to move away from that scary channel, even if you have to do so 50 times a day!

SWITCH IT!

CLICK IT!

MOVE AWAY!

CHANGE THE CHANNEL!

Staying there is the epitome of self-sabotage. You are literally allowing those images to live in your mind, invade your thoughts, and shape your reality. Remember how we talked about hope? Allowing hope to enter so you can see what's possible and evicting the negative thoughts that don't serve you are what will get you on the other side. Because you made room for something else that was possible.

Some say hope is not a strategy; I say hope *is* my strategy! Without hope you don't see another way. Hope ignites possibility. This doesn't happen on its own. True, hope alone won't save you. You still have to put in the effort. But let hope guide you versus fear. And allow faith to carry you through. You have to focus all your energy and intention to clean and maintain your Mental-Mind Channel.

STOP!

BREATHE!

REFOCUS!

Be an active participant in substituting your negative thoughts for positive ones. Don't get discouraged if it feels difficult at first. Reflexive ease comes with consistent practice. Did you learn how to ride a bike from the get-go, or did you fall a couple of times? You have to practice; put in the time to make your reality and your future better than it is now.

But even then don't fool yourself into thinking that if you practice it for a while, and it works, then you can now just sit back, relax, and take advantage of the benefits.

Changing the channel has to be synonymous to brushing your teeth every morning. Practice it daily ...

All the time.

Anywhere.

Regardless of the circumstances.

Take note! The fact that you are intentionally refocusing your thoughts doesn't mean that you are a drone devoid of feelings.

Let me give you an example:

I was really tired from working late in my office. I had an urgent report to complete before submitting it to a client. I did my best to work through the fatigue. I finally completed it and felt that warm feeling of accomplishment. Then suddenly, as if lightning struck, a thought flashed into my mind. "What if I made a mistake with any of the numbers?"

Rationally, I knew that I double-checked everything. I knew that I was meticulous, and I knew that my attention to detail was superb. That's rational. In reality, after pressing that Send button, a tsunami of thoughts washed into in my mind, creating unlikely scenarios that tricked me into believing I made errors in calculations.

So, what did I do? I focused my effort and attention on acknowledging that, yes, it is possible, but highly unlikely, I made an error. But I trust my work. Thus, I built into my mind an image of my report being received with great appreciation, reviewed, and approved. And I even saw myself having a pleasant conversation with that client to acknowledge the excellent work the report showed.

The report was accurate. My client was happy.

Was my report accurate because I changed the channel? No. It was accurate to begin with. But I did not allow myself to dwell in anxiety, self-doubt, worry, and negativity, which would have affected my sleep or my future productivity on other projects and simply robbed me of having peace of mind and even to potentially attract the deal to not get done because of manifesting the opposite of what I wanted just by the pure energy I was exuding. I chose to change the channel.

There's no magic to this. It's pure science. In computer science there is a term called GIGO (Garbage In, Garbage Out).

Translated, input your mind with garbage, then the behavioral output will be garbage. When you feed your mind instructions to bake a cake, then a cake it will bake! (Pardon my calorie-infused analogy, but cake is delicious, especially chocolate cake.) This knowledge isn't something I discovered, nor has it been kept a secret. This is common knowledge that has been around for thousands of years. Even the Bible acknowledges this: Book of Proverbs, 23:7: *"As a man thinketh in his heart, so is he."*

So why aren't more people privy to this information—and utilizing it? Some are. Pretty much every successful person you can think of uses the power of the subconscious to their advantage, in one way or another. Perhaps you can even recognize using this and it working to your advantage. Some call it prayer, others meditation, focus, mental health, hypnosis, visualization practice, or auto training, whatever name you want to put to it, it all has to do with how you use what God has gifted you (your subconscious) for your advantage to achieve your goals.

It changed my life. I would not be where I am today. I certainly would not be who I am if it weren't for the knowledge and practice of the power of using the subconscious for good. That is why I wrote this book to share with you, so you can apply it to your life. Share with friends, family, and even co-workers too.

Share your story with me. It is such an inspiration to hear the stories of how someone's life was transformed because I shared my story, my experience, and my approach to changing the channel. The truth is you always had it in you to transform your life. God created Mother Teresa and Albert Einstein the same way he did you and me. It all boils down to who chooses to use the resources we already have residing within, to tap into that power we hold. The power to change the thoughts that create our lives. To change the things we focus on in order to make room for what we truly want. To resist the evil that exists and refuse to hold space for the energies that don't serve you.

The highest achievers of real fulfillment figured out that happiness is not a destination. That you can create the life of your dreams by being willing to do what's required. Changing the channel to feel brave enough to take the action necessary is such a vital component to any success you want to achieve. Know your worth, standards, and boundaries. Be brave enough to stand up for yourself, no matter how intimidating. Because if you don't know your worth and you don't stand up for yourself, no one else will. And frankly, it is your responsibility. Forget about the what-ifs that don't serve you. What if this deal doesn't go through. What if I don't get the loan. etc. The next time you have a what-if moment, stop and counter that with *"What if it does work out? What if this is happening for me instead?"*

You are in the driver's seat. It's time to take the wheel and take what is yours. Start changing the things that you don't like ... one channel click at a time.

"Finally, brothers and sisters, whatever is true, whatever is noble, whatever is right, whatever is pure, whatever is lovely, whatever is admirable—if anything is excellent or praiseworthy—think about such things."

—*Philippians 4:8*

CHAPTER 7

A Time to Move, a Time to Be Still

As with everything, awareness is power. When you are aware of how your mindset and subconscious are affecting your well-being, you have the power to use that knowledge for good. You have to be able to distinguish between when it's time for you to steer, to put in the effort, to go hard after your goals, and when it is time to release the pedal, to calm your mind ... to slow down ... and focus on your inner peace.

Understanding this balance is vital for the equilibrium of your well-being, as anxiety and its variants are on the rise. As we discussed in Chapter 6, you have the power to switch the channel and take control more than you think. Because guess what? Anxiety is something you can overcome. Yes, I am speaking from experience. I learned this the hard way.

Take Control of Your Anxiety

Focusing on nothing else but the future triggers anxiety. Especially when it comes with a bunch of worse-case scenarios, of *what-ifs*. Answers to this hyper-focus reside somewhere in one's past experiences, with the root being either one or a combination of these factors: trauma, fear, stress, pressure.

Remember when we talked about F.E.A.R. (False Evidence Appearing Real)? Anxiety is greatly connected to that F.E.A.R., and it conjures feelings so powerful they cause you to believe the issues in focus are real. Feelings are not facts. Feelings stem from your thinking. Therefore, since you can change your thinking, you can most certainly change your feelings—including the feeling of anxiety.

Just think about it. You are about to interview for your dream job. You absolutely love everything about this job. You love the company, the corporate culture; you love what the position you're applying for is all about. Deep down you know you are qualified. You are excited about it, and you know it will be absolutely amazing to get the job. You feel you will do amazing if you are hired.

Wait ... Will you?

Will you ace the interview? Maybe you aren't qualified enough. You surely don't fit 100% of the job description, but you thought you could compensate with learning and experience in other areas. But then again maybe you don't have enough experience. Maybe you won't be able to apply your acquired knowledge. Maybe your interviewers will think you are overreaching. In fact, maybe they will think you are not a good fit and will wonder why you are even wasting their time in applying at all. What if you get hired ... but can't perform up to standard? What if you are wrong for the role? What if you feel like an imposter, hired for expectations you will never be able to fulfill?

Sounds familiar? This is imposter syndrome at its finest—creeping in, sparking anxiety, and making us second-guess ourselves. You start believing the lie that maybe this isn't for me, or that voice "I could never do that".

Yeah, I believe all of us have slid down that slippery steep slope. Maybe more than once or twice. The *you* in the example above all but talked yourself out from even going to the interview. And if you managed to go, the anxiety you created in your body will prevent you from performing to the best of your abilities. People can see and feel your anxiousness.

This is what F.E.A.R. is all about.

You know who you are. You know your capabilities; you know your worth; yet, that snowflake of doubt snowballed in an avalanche of anxiety. Make no mistake; anxiety can be quite crippling when you do not take control of it. It can spread like a virus in your body, and even transfer to others. Remember the last time someone's comment made you feel anxious, and you changed your course of action because of that anxiety? Me too!

It happens—at times to everyone.

We often feel like we are alone in these challenges and are the only one who has insecurities that plague our minds. But in reality, there are people, right now, in this very moment, going through the same things you are.

But here comes the good part! It doesn't have to be your reality. You have control over it. You can change it. You can overcome the feeling of anxiety. I know because I have done it. I already told you about my anxiety attacks and how I overcame that, but think about it for a moment—what is the best counteraction to anxiety?

You feel anxious ... mind racing ... palms sweating; you might experience palpitations or other physical reactions. How the hell do you stop that?

BREATHE

Most people fail to realize that they are literally holding their breath during an anxiety attack. This behavior causes you to hyperventilate, further exacerbating the other physical symptoms, which makes it difficult to calm your brain and your body. Let's do it now.

Stop and Breathe

Take 5 or even 10 deep breaths! I like to use the 5, 4, 6 second method. Breathe in for 5 seconds, hold for 4 seconds, and breathe out, slowly, for 6 seconds. Let's try it now. Start by breathing in slowly and deeply all the way, feel the air filling your lungs, in for 5, expand them to their capacity. Hold it for 4. Then ... slowly exhale for 6. Repeat.

Just something as simple as that will make an immediate difference.

Let's give your mind a new focus. Count from 1 to 10 and backward from 10 to 1.

Why does that work? Counting backward forces your brain to take mental control. When you do this you are activating the prefrontal cortex. Let's look at it further from a scientific point of view. You know I love data backed by science. When you encounter a stressor in your life (an external source, action, or an internal negative thought), the hypothalamus (the part of your brain responsible for keeping your body in balance) goes haywire. That, in turn, signals to your adrenal glands to overproduce adrenaline and cortisol (your stress hormone).

Why is that important? Well, in some instances, those two hormones can save your life because they are part of your fight-or-flight response; however, in normal circumstances, they just make your body overreact. Adrenaline, while not a "bad hormone" in general, in this circumstance is responsible for your increased heart rate and possibly higher blood pressure. Cortisol, which is dubbed the "stress hormone," increases your blood sugar and can suppress your digestive, growth, and reproductive systems.

In life-threatening circumstances, all of the above can be useful in saving your life. But if this surge of hormones happens in your body when there are no life-threatening circumstances present, and especially if it happens a lot (hello, even you type A, overachieving, controlling perfectionists!), it can damage your body and your mind.

The worse you feel, the more negative thoughts enter your brain and take residence in your subconscious, which causes you to feel even worse. Quite the Catch-22.

Let's face it; when you are experiencing anxiety, you actually are watering a slew of other problems to grow. Your immune system weakens, drowning in negativity as a result, making you more prone to infections. Chronic migraines, trouble sleeping, depression, and much more are some troublesome weeds of anxiety. It sounds crazy to believe anxiety can cause all of this.

So how does deep breathing help?

Taking a deep breath triggers the parasympathetic system (the counteraction of the fight-or-flight response). Counting backwards, overrides the amygdala, the brain's "alarm center" that triggers fear and panic. This activity also strengthens the pre-frontal cortex (your rational brain) ability to regulate emotional responses. Slower breathing also signals the parasympathetic nervous system (rest-and-digest) to calm the body. This helps your body literally hit a pause and reset. You will feel calmer, your heart rate and blood pressure will lower, and you will begin feeling better.

Of course, there are unexpected stressors that can exacerbate anxiety. When I am feeling nervous or anxious, I stay away from caffeine and alcohol, as I find those can be triggers. Same with refined sugar. You have to find out what triggers your response and try to control that as well.

As you can see, what I just covered are reactive tools to control your feeling of anxiety. Meaning when you feel anxious, these solutions are akin to putting a Band-Aid on the issue—likely a much deeper issue. As we know, Band-Aids eventually fall off ... bleeding continues, so to speak.

So, what is a proactive and productive way to deal with anxiety that will have long-term effects? Here's a similar, more detailed approach to the above:

1. Stop
2. Breathe
3. Clear your mind
4. Be still
5. Focus on positive thoughts
6. Make an image of you being calm, cool, and collected
7. Affirmations: While imagining being this exact thing you're saying:
   "*I am calm, cool, and collected.*" **Or** "*All is well, I am loved, and I am safe.*"
   Get creative!
8. Repeat

You can do this for as little as two to five minutes a day. Or as many times a day your schedule allows. Take note: Consistency is key. You have to make finding time to dedicate that time to yourself a must. Remember, secure your oxygen mask—first.

You overstressing and maintaining anxiety slowly exhaust your body. You aren't moving forward. You're no good to anyone, including yourself, when over-exhausted.

Let go of all impossible expectations from society, people, culture, and *you*. Looking at all those "perfect" vacations and perfect bodies social media feeds you, while you may have not seen a vacation in years, let alone wear a bathing suit confidently.

Get over it!

Life is not always picture-perfect. We are not perfect. Stop putting unrealistic expectations on yourself and others. You have to unload that stress. You don't need anyone's approval.

Let go of this facade of a "perfect" wife (husband), mom, father, teacher, business leader, sister, daughter, and so on.

Accept yourself with all your imperfections. Let go of what you did in the past. Or what you didn't do, could've done. It's in the past. What matters is now, right now! There are so many great people in this life who didn't start until their 60s or beyond. But they did it. So, you can too! Today you will start your new life with this profound belief that you already have what it takes to change your life. It starts right NOW. Today. You are your greatest asset, literally. You are uniquely you. No one else is like YOU. Surround yourself with people who support and love you, who grow with you, and accept you for who you are. And know that you are not alone when you are struggling. Find your village, your tribe, and stick with them.

Unmet obligations often give rise to anxiety. Be intentional about how you structure your work and organize your responsibilities (activities). Being disorganized or procrastinating can induce anxiety. This can be a tough pill to swallow for procrastinators (hello, me!), but it is true. I was there before always pushing things to the very last minute only causing unnecessary stress. The amount of anxiety you can induce just by delaying what you have to do can feel unbearable. Not to mention ... it is self-induced, thus completely preventable. That is why I say awareness is half the battle. The power to control where you place your focus of attention and the thoughts you entertain change how you feel.

Repeat after me: "*I can control my thoughts, and that will change how I feel.*"

Get Moving

You know what else will change how you feel? Moving your body! You probably have heard it a thousand times, but exercise is one of the best ways to combat stress. Physical activity positively impacts not only the body but the mind as well. That is why it's one of the best proactive approaches to combat anxiety. While breathing techniques and meditation are excellent rescue remedies, exercise is like your daily dose of vitamins that contribute to keeping you healthy, happy, and anxiety free.

You don't have to be a marathon runner to keep your body healthy. I'm not. I am way far from the most exercise-crazy person; but I understand the value of knowing when to move my body. Even climbing the stairs of your home, or parking farther from the store entrance (unless you are in heels, of course!) so you can take those extra steps, makes a difference.

Whenever my ideal parking spot is unavailable, I remind myself that this is to my benefit and how grateful I am that I am healthy enough to walk (especially on days I skipped a workout). The absence of my ideal parking spot is another example of seeing even the *smallest* of obstacles as opportunities or blessings. This change in perception makes it easier for me to maintain my mental regulation, instead of being that crazy person, driving around in circles, predatorily hunting for that precious open VIP space, right next to the entrance. Come on; you know what I'm talking about!

More times than not though I get that VIP parking. *"Oh mommy is with us. So we'll definitely get the best parking,"* my kids always say when I am with them, and daddy is driving. This powerful demonstration of manifesting is now a running family joke! What's my secret you ask? I verbalize—with truth and gratitude—this statement, *"I always get the best parking!"* I said it so much that it became my reality! Without exaggeration. Anyone who knows me is aware that, I do always get the best parking, even when it is the middle of a parking riot.

Exercise is not a once-a-month pill. You have to build it into your lifestyle cycle. It's not whether you feel like exercising or not. It is about discipline. Don't just set a goal to exercise—commit to it. It's your commitments that will carry you further than the goal itself. It's that simple. Do not complicate it. Ask ANY successful human who does this consistently. Exercise has to become a part of *who* you are.

Find any type of exercise that resonates with you and your lifestyle. Maybe you like dancing; maybe you like tennis; maybe you like running on a treadmill or outdoor exclusive activities; maybe you like lifting weights or yoga, Pilates, Tae-Kwon-Do, Tai Chi ... you name it. Try and see what hits home with you. That's the start to making lasting change.

Don't wait to have the right leggings, or be in the right mood, or sign up for a class, or buy that expensive piece of equipment. Don't wait until you feel like doing it. Half the time I don't feel like doing it either. But I know if I commit, I must show up. I only hurt myself if I don't. Do it right now! It can be a small step on your bedroom floor, doing sit-ups or squats. Heck do squats in the shower! I've done plenty of this as a gap filler. No excuses. This will bring the flood of energy you need to make the next step. Ancient philosopher, Lao Tzu, said, *"The journey of a thousand miles begins with a single step."*

Make no mistake; when we are talking about a results-driven mindset, you don't have to want to do it (whatever it is) every single time. But you have to commit; you have to make the decision. A lot of times, people wait to do something. It's expressed in their language, "I would like, I want to, I wish ..." If that something will create the results you want, don't wait. Commit today. Do it. Change your life by taking this small step that will lead to bigger and better things. Change "I want to" to *"I need to. I am doing it—today!"*

It's not just exercise that is important for prevention where feelings of anxiety and stress are concerned. I was inspired to develop this framework demonstrating the important relationship between your body, mind, and stomach. My mom is often asked how she stays looking so young. She is 81 and people never believe her age. She taught me the importance of the triangle—the holy trinity of good living—your mind, stomach, and heart.

A healthy gut is one of the best things you can do to improve your mental health, and to help eliminate presenting issues—if any exist. This is backed by research.

Behold, the Holy Trinity of Good Living!

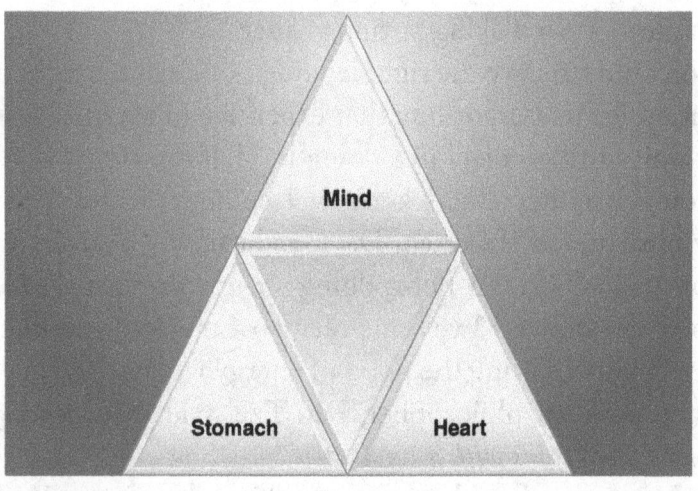

"Do you not know that your bodies are temples of the Holy Spirit... Therefore honor God with your bodies."
—1 Corinthians 6:19-20

What you feed your mind, what you feed your stomach, and what you feed your heart are what builds or destroys you. So take caution with what you feed your mind, stomach, and heart. Here is a recipe for spiritual disaster. Feed your mind negative thoughts, maintain a horrid diet, and feed your heart anger, resentment, and bitterness. Take note: What you feed your mind influences how your stomach reacts. Your stomach is akin to a second brain. In fact, it is called the enteric brain. There is a gut brain connection via your vagus nerve, which influences your emotions and even the decisions you make. Your gut also has a microbiome impact. The bacteria in your gut produce chemicals, which in turn impacts your stress levels and even your immune system.

In the same way, when you feed your mind positive thoughts, bathe yourself with good feelings such as love, acceptance, and forgiveness. When you eat healthy, it all contributes to building and maintaining the holistic totality of your life. Here is a fun fact: Over 90% of your serotonin (that good feeling neurotransmitter) is produced in your gut. Astonishing, isn't it?

Keep this triangle at the center of your day-to-day life, so it becomes a reminder of what you need to maintain. It is your responsibility to control what goes in and what needs to go out. No one else but you. How often have you felt so motivated because you went to a seminar or you did that training and you feel so pumped and ready to take on the world!? But wait, a week or two or three goes by and now that motivation wears off, starts to fade. Why is this? Because you did not maintain it. You have to maintain it just like anything else in life. When you buy that beautiful car, you drive it off the lot, it works great, you feel good, you have a functional car and it might even smell nice and new. Then months or years go by and if you don't take it in for service, it will eventually break down. Same with your mind, body, and what you feed yourself. This is how I want you to think about your life. Your mind, heart, and stomach. It is all connected.

Mental Detox

I cannot stress enough how important mental detox is for your well-being and for moving you in the direction of your dreams. A clouded mind is like a muddy river. You put your hand in to search for gold, only pull out a half-chewed shoe. I want to share with you the mental detox practices that I use. This list is not exhaustive. But any practice that helps you clear your mind and stay focused is good for you.

Here is what I do:

- **Unplug**

    You heard that right. Digital overload is one of the nemeses of mental health, so digital detox is one of the top practices on my list. Do it the way you feel works for you—whether unplugging from social media or TV, or going without a phone for an unspecified amount of time. Designate areas in your home that are a technology-free zone. When I did this with my family it was a total game-changer. You can start small. Maybe it is just as simple as not checking your emails after you get home from work. Practicing digital unplugging opens up mental spaces in your mind for you to think and to psychologically breathe. This has even been proven to help poor sleep patterns, too.

- **Gratitude Journal**

    I have a gratitude journal that helps me the most to focus on a clearer picture for my future. If I am worried about my health, I write, "Thank you, God, for my strong and healthy body." If my mind is spinning, I write, "Thank you for the peace that tomorrow will bring." If I am nervous about something, "I am grateful for feeling peace during the storm" and "This too shall pass." The pattern is to simply counteract the worry that you feel with the opposite of what you would like to feel if you can turn it around right now. And even when things are going well. I'm just reflecting on the good in my life. I write, "Thank you for my children. Thank you for my husband's unconditional love. Thank you to God and my faith." Whatever feels right for you. It is so nurturing to your soul.

    I also journal, putting down on paper what it is that I want to manifest more of in my life. I am a great mother; I am a fabulous wife. I am a great leader. (This book is a #1 New York Times best seller! Let's see if this one comes true!) And so forth. Remember, what you feel you will attract more of. If you need answers to a challenge, get it out of your head and clear your mind so you can focus on solutions for the things that you can change.

- **Take a "friends and family" vacation**

    Audit your circle of people. That friend or family member who you call and they always have something they're complaining about. You know who those people are in your lives. It cannot be your every day or you will be consumed by it. There have been studies that have that the five people you are around the most will become your reality. You will pick up on their habits, their complaining, or their limited mindsets. And guess what else? Their gut bacteria. This one is weird. A 2019 study in *Nature* found that cohabiting individuals share more similar micro-biomes than those who don't live together, if they're around them long enough. What? This was the hardest thing for me to believe I have to say. So don't freak out. Just pay attention to the people you spend your time with.

    Make a list of the people who you communicate with the most. Write down what kind of influence these people have on your mood, your mind, and your body. Next step? Try to reduce communication and interactions with the ones who don't grow you in a positive way. I understand that there are certain family dynamics where you can't completely cut off someone who brings negative energy, but the least you can do is limit your exposure or their duration. Surround yourself with love and support instead. Don't get me wrong—there's a time and place to show empathy and grace, even for friends or family who are struggling or reckless. But know your limits. Constant exposure to negativity will affect you more than you realize.

- **Embrace the outdoors**

    Being in nature can bring about a calm mental state. Explore how different environments affect you. A walk by the beach, a hike, a swim ... even if you go outside of your home, in your yard or your deck, let the sun hit your face, forget the sunglasses. Go outside on your grass barefoot if you can. Did you know by going outside barefoot you will receive the best kind of grounding, naturally? You won't need those mats (we have some) but now I do my best to receive it naturally from nature. Let the feeling of the warm sun remind you where you came from. Soak up the vitamin D. Find your nature fix and whatever works for you.

- **Take a "Me, Myself, and I" day**

    This is my favorite one. No matter how much you love your family, how adorable your kids are, and how loving your spouse is, there comes a time when you just need a minute. Don't wait for that time. Schedule a date with yourself and enjoy it to the fullest extent to reconnect with yourself and your inner peace. Get that massage. Take yourself shopping. It does not have to be elaborate. It can be you doing nothing but eating popcorn and binge-watching your guilty pleasure TV show ... and be guilt free from doing it. It can be you sleeping in, because you never get to. Or reading that book you didn't get to finish. Making a new recipe without a million interruptions. Whatever it is make sure it is something for YOU, that you enjoy doing.

- **Improve your inner conversation**

    How you talk to yourself is equally as important. Use language that is loving, supportive, and caring when you are talking to and about yourself. Language that doesn't serve you? Show it the door. Never use negative or disparaging phrases when you are addressing yourself or your actions.

Focus on what is good, even if it needs improvement. I see it as another form of affirmation. "I am worthy of love," "I am happy," "I am calm, cool, and collected," "I can do anything I set my mind to," "I always meet the right people," "I always find time for myself." The more you say this the more you will experience that of which you just said.

Peace

I believe that meditation deserves its own space when we are talking about practices that bring health and prosperity into our lives. But it is sad so many people connect meditation with the image of it being a fad, because of the many buzzwords connected to it—spiritual practice, mindfulness, mind-body awareness, etc.

At the end of the day, meditation, to me, is that moment of connection between one's mind, body, and soul; when your mind is quiet, your body becomes still, and your soul is free.

We have so many teachings and app options that are supposed to promote the best meditation practices. This is good as it makes this practice accessible to the public. However, with so many options to choose from it's no wonder purchase paralysis overwhelms people, thus making it harder to start one's meditation.

Let me make it clear—you can practice meditation ANYTIME, ANYWHERE.

You don't need any special knowledge, equipment, environment, or clothes (trust me, I have heard it all) to practice calming your mind and reconnecting with your spirit. You also don't need to spend hours in a meditative state to reap the benefits.

A meditation can be short—3–5 minutes—or longer, if you have the desire or time. You can do it while standing in line at the grocery store, or in the car waiting in traffic (just don't close your eyes), or when you are on hold with customer service (ain't that the truth!), virtually anywhere. Yes, being still in a quiet place is best; but keep in mind that it does not have to be. Work with what you have.

You can practice meditation in any position, standing, sitting, or lying down ... whatever works for you and your lifestyle.

Mastering your self-focus, breathing, and relaxation takes practice, of course, as with everything. But the benefits are undeniable, especially when you connect your meditative practices with the spiritual connection you have with a higher being, by adding prayer or religious reflection.

I want to bring to your attention two meditations that I created specifically for you. One is focused on relaxation, the other one on inspiration. Use these two techniques to get a taste of the results you can achieve. Then alter the content the way you feel is most beneficial to you. While you can do this anywhere, I want to encourage you to do these in a quiet space.

Meditation for Relaxation:

Find a quiet place where you can be still.

Turn your phone off (trust me, it can wait 10 minutes if that is all you have).

Take a deep breath in for 5, 4, 3, 2, 1 through your nose slowly and hold it for 4, 3, 2, 1, and release it slowly for 6, 5, 4, 3, 2, 1.

Close your eyes and relax your shoulders and body, letting everything go.

Repeat the above breathing exercise two more times, and then just allow yourself to drift off into relaxation, breathing normally.

As you are doing this, go to a place in your mind where you find relaxation. Maybe it is you on the beach alone or with a loved one. It could be at a park by a tree. It can be anywhere you choose.

Allow your mind to feel that moment you have imagined, as if you are there now.

Feel the wind blowing against your cheek.

Feel every part of your body going deeper into relaxation.

Feel your heartbeat through every breath you take.

Hear the sounds of the waves crashing or the birds chirping. Maybe it is the sound of rain. Stay in this moment, breathing ever so gently and relaxing.

Notice how relaxed you are feeling now that you have quieted your mind to relax even more.

You can do this meditation for 5 minutes or longer. The effects are immediate. You can even do this if you feel stressed or anxious. But do it proactively; don't wait until you feel stressed. You can do it anywhere. Be creative and work with what you have. I promise you will feel relaxed and at peace.

Meditation for Inspiration:

Find a place where you can be still.

Close your eyes, and take a deep breath, slowly in through your mouth, then breathe out through your nose.

Repeat the above two times, *slowly* to center yourself.

As you breathe you become centered with your mind and body.

Notice your breath as you feel your heartbeat, focus on the feeling of your heartbeat and your shoulders relaxing.

Now, imagine where you want to be. What goal do you have? It could be small or big. What does attaining that goal look like?

See it. Where are you?

Who are you with?

What does it sound like?

Now that you have achieved this goal, what are you now able to do as a result of making that happen?

See it as if you're *already* there doing it!

Keep those images bright and loud so you can begin to experience it and feel it with your every being.

Keep breathing with your eyes closed as you imagine what's possible.

End your mediation with a "thank you," because it is already on its way to you.

The duration of the practice is up to you. For example, from 5 minutes up to 30 minutes. Be as creative as you like. When you're done you will feel more motivated than when you started. Because you have selected those feelings of joy and accomplishment for whatever it is that you're meditating on. It can be anything. That meeting with that important contact you have. It can be the big goal to double your business. A vacation in Italy. You feeling your best. Or a great time with your family at dinner. Anything at all. Same recipe.

You are the architect of your life. When you imagine and visualize what you want, you give your brain a target. The universe will respond to what you focus on time and time again. It never fails.

"Do not be anxious about anything ... present your requests to God."
—Philippians 4:6–7

CHAPTER

8

God's Daily Dosage

I remember when I was a single mom in my mid-20s, experiencing success for the first time in real estate. It came with its ups and downs. I had this inner pulling where I began to feel so thirsty for answers, spiritually. I believe it was God's way of talking to me. I attended numerous different churches varying in faiths, all in search of something more. I grew up Catholic. And I remember even as a teenager challenging my parents as to why we adopted the Catholic faith.

"If Judaism was the first religion, why are we not Jewish?" I asked. Maybe not so expected from a 13-year-old at the time.

This inquisitive trait served me later in life while searching for a new and suitable church for my kids and me. I was yearning for answers.

In my search I stumbled across a church where later my connection to the Holy Spirit deepened. The Bible and its teachings enthralled me. I was obsessed with learning how scripture brings healing during difficult times. My mom always read the Bible to us in Spanish when we were kids, which I did not fully understand. Later I realized what I missed out on. It's interesting that when we seek, we will find. Often, I found myself seeking answers, but I did not always know answers to what, exactly. And I would often find them in teachings of the Bible. Scriptures. I do believe that having God in your life is like that daily vitamin D we all need from the sun. This is not some sort of luxury; it is a necessity to survive life. To prosper, to propel forward.

The truth is, God lives in all of us. You already have a dose of God inside of you daily. It is made available to you when you're open to receive. Because spirituality is an intimate and personal exploration, individual interpretations of God and belief systems widely differ. My relationship with Our Creator is simple: I believe in God, and in return, I allow God to work miracles in my life. It is the essence of where faith is born. This reciprocal belief empowers me through adversity, fuels my inspiration, and confirms and reassures me that I'm fulfilling my guided purpose.

Whether you are religious or not, I believe the words that I am about to share with you in this chapter apply to anyone, of any religion, with any interpretation of God. You can still gain inspiration and strength from the daily practice of prayer, in any form that appeals to you. Believing in a higher purpose other than yourself nourishes your soul. If you are hesitant, I'm not one to convince you otherwise. However, I challenge you to let go of the wheel of what you're trying to control, the struggle that you may be walking through right now and surrender it to God.

I remember holding on to the wheel so tightly when dealing with a health scare, until I finally let go of the wheel because I felt God's presence telling me that it was okay, because I asked God for strength. I asked God to take over, and he did. Alone we do nothing, with God all things are possible. I have lived this now too many times than I can count and know without fail that I owe everything to my mom for teaching me that with God all things are in fact possible. My mom instilled this in me at a young age. She showed me what perseverance was when you allow the faith in God into your life.

My father overcame cancer five times, even Stage (3) lung cancer. Though it sidelined him, my father fought with a faith in God bigger than the diagnosis. Dad never let his setback define him. In the end though, it was his lifestyle that caught up with him.

My father is no longer with us; but what stays with me is his example: no matter what you face, it's you who decides whether it defeats you, or you rise to the occasion and fight.

During that difficult time, my mom had $15 to her name; yet, she managed to stretch it to feed us. Mom made tamales, and my three siblings and I went around our apartment complex selling them by the dozen, door to door. (Talk about sales training early on!) To our surprise, the money multiplied. When I asked my mom, how she did it, she simply said, *"With God on our side, anything is possible."*

And through that, I learned firsthand how faith doesn't just carry you through—it moves you to action, during the hardest moments.

Only you can say if you've experienced the presence of God in your life. Don't despair if you haven't discovered it yet. God does not need you to be perfect. He meets you right where you are. Adopt the thoughts and practices in this chapter to your circumstances and understanding of God, and you'll be on your way to having a deeper connection to your higher power and self that will help you to build your faith through life's challenging moments.

Your God-Given Potential

I can't stay silent when someone tells me that their current struggle is their fate, or worst of all, they are "unlucky." God created you—called you a masterpiece!—composed of all your unique gifts and imperfections, He gave you a powerful mind and brain. Yes, things can happen and yes, we go through pain, real pain. God is doing something far greater than you can see. And now it has become your story of how you gained resilience from it but that does not mean that it is your fate and you cannot change it. Oftentimes, they can change. Our pain always comes with a deeper meaning that we use later in life. It may be a tough season; but it is never your fate where you are trapped in your struggle.

God built in you free will to do whatever you desire. God gave you the power of choice. You get to decide if you'll walk a straight line, or not. God won't protect you from making mistakes. The greatest tool you hold, which no amount of money can buy, is your mind. With this you can truly create the life you want. You get to decide if you surrender to circumstance, or persevere, challenging what could be. You can make rational (and some irrational) decisions, learn from your mistakes, improve, grow, and do amazing things.

Your brain is like a quantum supercomputer with infinite power that can explore millions of opportunities at the same time. Your brain possesses immense power to bring you to a great place (think rainbows and butterflies), or take you to that dark, unending spiral of self-pity, where excuses masquerade as wallpaper, and anxiety and fear weave themselves into a carpet.

God wants you to succeed. God wants you to live life to your fullest potential. However, it's not God's job to get you there. So while you can receive strength, inspiration, and grace from our

Creator when you ask, it is *you* who is ultimately responsible for your life, your decisions, and your actions. Grabbing the wheel to take the action necessary is vital as is knowing when to let go of the wheel and let God do the work because you asked for help and because of what you are in alignment with.

Which one do you find yourself currently practicing?

- You have given up on your dreams and maybe are even wallowing, asking, "Why me?"

Or:

- You are putting faith in your higher power, knowing that although you may not see results right away, you are always being divinely guided in the perfect timing that is best suited for you.

You have a beast of an "off-road vehicle" in your body and mind. True, bruises and a few scratches here and there might occur, but you have everything you need to arrive at your destination intact. When bumps on the road surprise you ... switch gears. When you pop a tire, change it. Most people give up after experiencing obstacles, but God did not create you to have weak sense of conviction and fealty.

The fact that you carry within yourself the potential God gave you, the same as every other person on Earth who has succeeded, doesn't mean you won't face challenges. You are molded for resilience. God gave *you* the tools (your brain and your subconscious) to control the things in your life and create the life you dream of.

That's how life is—a package deal; the fear, the joy, the disappointment, and resilience come from living life with free will. Imagine if you never had a reason to have faith? No reason to lean on God and allow your faith to grow. Imagine if you never had to experience resilience? You have been given all the ingredients to be whoever you want to be. God, however, is not going to do it for you. He's not looking for laziness; He wants you to knock on the door and ask for what you want, and to lean on him when you feel weak. You are never alone; He lives within you. He won't take the first step for you; but He will give you the strength needed to do so because you asked. You will still feel His spirit energizing and supporting you.

Love is a necessary tool for success!

Think about it this way: There are two people, both from the same background, same education, and same family fortune, etc. One succeeds, only to become a world-renowned professor; the other succumbs to drugs and loses his money.

Why?

If we are using just plain logic, both were given an equal start, equal opportunities. Why did one succeed and the other one didn't? Because each of us embraces our God-given power and our prime opportunities differently, especially when faced with challenges. How you face challenges, and the decisions that follow, defines what you will become, how you will succeed, and the life that you will have. Your attitude in the face of intimidating challenges, and the consequential decisions that follow, defines what and *who* you become, most importantly, *how* you will succeed, and the life you will lead. You have to be impervious to rejection and possess infinite amounts of self-love that sustains you throughout the predictable darkest times. You also need to accept and empower yourself with Our Creator's blessing and grace, so that you can continue striving to be better than your best!

We have talked about this time and again in previous chapters. If you don't like the movie ... "change the channel"!

So if:

- You are unhappy and unfulfilled? Change the channel!
- You are sick and tired of failing? Change the channel!
- You are wallowing in negativity and cheap talk? Change the channel!
- You are crumbling because of rejection? Change the channel!

No one else, not even your mom can do that for you. Truth is it all boils down to what you are focusing on and keeping alive. Think of your thoughts as the steering wheel of your life, wherever you point it is where you will go. Whatever you think about most is what will dictate your life. Which is why above I mentioned "changing the channel." It allows you to break that pattern of focus so you can get more—more of what you want versus what you don't want.

Ask, and You Shall Receive

Ask, and it shall be given to you;
seek, and ye shall find; knock,
and it shall be opened unto you.

—Matthew 7:7

This is one of my favorite verses. I use this time and time again. My closest friends tell me, "You always get what you want," and I tell them, yes I do. Even when I want something and it doesn't happen, I am still getting what I want. Something better is coming. See the difference? How freeing is that? I used to worry, no obsess, when things did not work out. Now, with this new perspective I allow things to flow openly and freely. Someone recently told me, "I prayed so hard that I don't want to be in debt anymore, and here, God is staying silent to my prayer."

So, let me get this straight. You prayed to God about what you *didn't* want, and you didn't get what you wanted? Did you tell God what you want instead? Or were you focusing on what it is that you DON'T want instead?

Because the message here is clear—*ask, and you shall receive*. What did you ask for? What do you want? Or what *don't* you want? God is not interested in hearing what you don't want. Correspondingly, you don't want your subconscious to hear what you don't want either, or that is exactly what it will pay attention to and deliver on.

What is it that YOU DO WANT?

Matthew 7:7 is my favorite scripture because it clearly defines what is expected from you—ASK, and then you shall RECEIVE. Oh, but wait! Couple this with BELIEF, and it will be done. Plain and simple.

- ✓ Don't ask to not lose your house; ask for the wisdom to see the path that will help you find a better solution.
- ✓ Don't ask for money; ask to start or grow your business. Ask to have the means to travel with your kids to show them other cultures. Ask for financial security.
- ✓ Don't ask to not lose your relationship; ask for the wisdom to make your relationship better.

Ask from a place of possibility that moves you forward, instead of performing from a place of debilitating fear, which defeats you.

The truth is you are *constantly* asking for what you want, *and* what you don't want, even if you're consciously unaware of it. Remember the frequencies of your vibrational energy? That is why being intentional in your self-talk also matters. In fact, it is vital. You set the expectations.

If you are asking, "What if I am not worthy or good enough?" Or say, "I don't deserve this," "I can never do that" ... Then guess what? You are clearly sending a message that you are unworthy, and you will never do that. So why not use this natural mind hack that's in your favor to ask for what you actually want in your life? Oh, and by the way, this "mind hack" comes from Our Creator. God wants to know the desires of your heart. As this scripture puts it clearly—*James 4:2*—*You do not have because you do not ask.*

During my self-discovery, I was so happy being single and working on myself. I did not even crave a relationship. People at my office would always tell me that I had everything so great in my life, why don't I have a boyfriend. And I remember so vividly responding, "I don't have time for a boyfriend. Relationships require work." (Limiting belief.) Or I would say, the people I meet are not on my level because I'm so driven and have dreams while others I meet do not.

Don't get me wrong; I knew that one day I would remarry. I knew it with such faith; I just didn't want it at that time. Then, I left for a conference, and my mom dropped me off at the airport. As I got out of the car and said good-bye, I said, *"Who knows, I may meet my future husband where I'm going."* I have never gone on a work trip and mixed business with pleasure—ever. It was a real estate conference. My husband has nothing to do with the real estate business and had no business being there. But talk about manifesting your words. They have power.

Years before I met my husband I said to myself (self-talk) that by the time I was in my mid-30s I would have two more children—boys—back-to-back; maybe a year or two apart. True story! Why did I say that? I already had two kids; you might think I was crazy to want to start over. I knew that I wanted to do it again, only this time I was going to do it the right way.

I remember two sons of one of my clients and thinking how cool it was seeing two boys so close in age. And literally years later this became my reality. Why? Because I put something out there. Can you look back at something you said and then it happened? Coincidence? I think not.

Remember that saying, be careful what you wish for? That is not a joke. Words have meaning. Couple that with conviction. You'll be a mega manifesto!

I remember vividly one of my sales training sessions. Sales reps were about to do a presentation they intended to pitch to a prospective client. The presentations were not just interesting, but well-made too. The students clearly demonstrated competence for the products and services they were intending to pitch; yet, something was missing.

I turned around and asked, "What is the outcome that you want from your client meetings?" I heard many different answers:

- "I want to understand my client's needs better."
- "I want my clients to understand our services."
- "I want to build rapport with my contact."

True, to build a strong client relationship all of the above are crucial in the sales process. However, take note: None of these is the actual outcome, the end goal that anyone in sales should have had in mind when walking through their customers' conference room doors. Closing the deal, signing the contract, winning the client, earning their business, whatever you want to call it, *is* the end goal, the intention in the sales process, where it's *tangible*; yet, no one realized this.

In any aspect of life this is true. Sometimes we get so entwined in the details that we miss the bigger picture. Think about what it is that you want; what is it that your heart desires. What is your most sincere and heartfelt prayer about? Are you asking for what you really want? Or are you wrapping your wishes in stifling insecurity that, at day's end, even God can't figure out what it is that you truly want?

This reminds me of the scene from *Bruce Almighty* with Jim Carey. At the end of the movie, God asks Bruce what he wants. Bruce starts talking about world peace and hungry children. God stops him and asks him to give him a real prayer from the heart, not a pageant speech from Miss America. Bruce thinks for a moment and then says to God that he doesn't want his lover back; he just wants her to find happiness and be loved as she truly deserves. With that selfless act, he elicits from God, "Now that's a prayer!"

Being selfless, kind, loving, and compassionate are true virtues to embody so we grow. This scene from a movie illustrates how we sometimes try to be who we think God wants us to be, instead of being who we are—real humans with real flaws, having real feelings, real wants and desires, and who learn real lessons. God always knows who we are. We don't need to tell him that.

If we need help, we need to ask for what we want.

The Power of Prayer

If you have experienced the power of prayer firsthand, I don't need to convince you that it's real. If you haven't, then that moment when you realize the truth, feel it, and witness it, that feeling of your first time is priceless. Living God's truth is possible for all of us. And we should be thankful to Our Creator for it.

We all experience challenges in our lives, ones that test this power. Sometimes these challenges force us to confront our faith, our conviction, and our strength. That is why it is so important that we set our intention every day with the power of prayer as well. Just think about this, when you pray, how do you actually pray? What does your voice sound like in your head? Are you using empowering words? Are you utilizing words that inspire instead of diminish? Is it a prayer of hope or one of fear? Does it move you forward, or does it only confirm the very thing you want to run away from (the thing you fear the most)?

Maybe a better question to ask yourself is this: When was the last time you prayed? I mean *really* prayed. Was it the moment you felt scared and didn't know what else to do? It's okay if this is you. There is absolutely no shame in asking for God's help when you're in trouble. However, it is about learning and acknowledging that when you allow God to live in you, every day, in *everything* you do, you start to live and thrive with a greater sense of comfort. You know that no matter what happens, you're *never* alone. You now walk, allowing faith to guide you, versus fear. With GOD, anything, and I truly mean ANYTHING is possible.

In 2021 a group of scientists performed comparatively experimental studies[1] on the neuro-cognitive and physiological changes in humans during prayer. They discovered that prayer influenced not only human neuro-activity but also had physiological benefits as well. In the conclusion of the study, the scientists pointed out that physiological changes in blood pressure, heart and respiratory rate, as well as cardiovascular activity, were detected. The benefits of the power of prayer were undeniable—improved mental and physical health, as well as improved mental function, control, and pain tolerance.

Your conversation with God, your spiritual practice with Our Creator, or with whatever understanding you have about the Universal Beginning, is an important factor in your overall well-being. Feeling pure of heart and extending authentic Thank You to Our Creator extends a positively charged vibration around you, hugging you. Your physical health and mental well-being improve too.

---

[1] Chin, F., Chou, R., Waqas, M. et al. (2021). Efficacy of prayer in inducing immediate physiological changes: a systematic analysis of objective experiments. *Journal of Complementary and Integrative Medicine* 18 (4): 679–684. https://doi.org/10.1515/jcim-2020-0075.

It is important in your prayer to God to focus on the positive aspects of *any* situation. Thank Our Creator for all the blessings in your life, and by golly, there are many! Even if you are at the bottom at this moment; perhaps you're struggling, or in physical or mental pain, find something to be thankful for. For instance, if you just woke up, be thankful that you had a place to sleep and have healthy lungs today. That you're BREATHING!

Have a prayer with grace, not a pity party. The latter doesn't give God a fighting chance to help you. If you are negative, constantly doubting your worth, and ignoring everything that's going right, this is self-sabotage. Now, don't get me wrong. Being in pain, feeling like there is no pathway out, or a solution, doesn't mean you must ignore your vulnerability, and fake your way through prayer. Hear me out. True prayer moves you forward. At times you may not know what to say. But surrendering, having grace is all it takes, getting on your knees when you feel, weak, broken, and saying, "God, I feel weak. Give me the strength." Or, "God, I feel lost. Give me clarity. Guide me on what I should do." The point is ... you can be broken, and yet still move toward what you want. I give these examples because I lived it. I still do.

I don't believe God answers prayers about self-sabotaging. Think about it; we are all created in God's likeness. Why would He create something unworthy? God wants to help you. God is there for you, but you have to *allow* God within you to do it. Doing the work requires you to let go of the wheel, and trust that God is working miracles in your life right now. Because you asked, because you believed God would. Because you are showing up and doing your part.

We have heard the anecdote about the person who was a victim of a deadly flood, crouched on his/her rooftop and praying for God's help.

I've dramatized it, somewhat (Yes, I love movie dramas) ...

EXT. FLOODED AREA—DAY

VICTIM, perched on his rooftop, frightened by the flooding, lightning and torrential rains ... prays to God.

A boat passes by. Victim ignores it

> VICTIM
> (To boat captain)
> I don't need it. God is going to help me. Thank you.

A helicopter passes overhead. The victim ignores it

> VICTIM
> (To helicopter pilot)
> I don't need it. God is going to help me. Thank you.

Numerous land, air, and flood-based vehicles come to Victim's aid, offering their help. Same story ... Victim ignores their generous and lifesaving offers.

Well, guess what? Victim drowns. And ...

EXT. HEAVEN—DAY

Beautiful, sunshine illuminates. Cotton ball-like clouds bounce everywhere.

> VICTIM
> God, I believe in you so much
> I prayed to you so much.
> Why didn't you save me?

> GOD
> Well, I sent you a boat and a helicopter ...
> What else do you want me to do?

This is so unbelievably true! God sometimes answers our prayers in disguise and maybe at times, we don't listen. He is there to help you, regardless of your messy state of mind and life circumstances. You must participate in your success. Nothing is going to land on your lap. Don't expect life or Our Creator to offer you something while you wallow in self-pity. Invest in yourself.

What message are you delivering to your subconscious if you are constantly complaining and saying you are unworthy or that nothing in your life is working? Sure, life can be hard at times. Fall down, cry yourself to sleep if needed; but then get back up! Stand up, rise, and go again!

Distance yourself from your negative feelings. Instead of saying, "I am weak," say instead, "I *feel* weak; God help me to feel better." Not long ago my son came home from school and told me he was mad. I immediately redirected him, "No, my love. You are not mad; you are FEELING mad." This statement reframe made an immediate difference because you are addressing the behavior instead of focusing on the person. When you say, "*I am*," you are attaching your identity to the expressed behavior. I am frustrated; no, you *feel* frustrated.

When you seize the opportunity to teach your kid when they get into trouble, you don't want to say, "You are bad"; instead, address the *behavior*. It works wonders. It empowers the child to change because changing a behavior is easy, but changing a personality is not. This same strategy works on adults too.

The Power of "The Word"

Scriptures correlate with life in such a way that we can learn from them. They also enrich our spiritual experiences too.

The Power of Positive Thinking provided me an alternate perspective toward my private prayer habits. No matter the medium of your spiritual connection practice, a conversation with Our Creator gives you an intimate insight into what can be yours, via a more positive experience based on controlling your thoughts and refocusing them for good.

The biggest gift that God has given you, along with the power of free will, is the power to control your thoughts. By now you already are aware of this.

Purposeful Prayer

Leaving yourself on autopilot doesn't free yourself from God; you are still tethered to Him, and you are still subconsciously "asking" for what you want. But if you haven't designed your request with intention, then your prayers, your meditation, and any other spiritual practice will bring you just that—autopilot results.

We aren't talking about accidental grace here. We are talking about fulfilling your God-given potential in any part of your life—via *deliberate intention*. If a thought inhabits your mind, it better be positive; that's what I always say.

Remember: You have control over what you feed your *mind*, your *heart*, just as you do with your *stomach*.

I've prepared a list of scriptures to equip you for whatever you may be going through right now. Even if everything is going right, I love to remind myself of these scriptures. I hope these can provide you with ideas on how to incorporate spiritual practices in setting your intentions. Feel free to work on adding other scriptures in a similar manner to your prayer.

Scriptures

The following scriptures are ones that have gotten me through the toughest of times. And allowed the success I experienced to gain even more momentum. My hope is that you will find peace and encouragement in them too.

For Love: *"God is love. Whoever lives in love lives in God, and God in them."* ***1 John 4:16***

For Peace: *"Peace I leave with you; my peace I give you. I do not give to you as the world gives. Do not let your hearts be troubled and do not be afraid."* ***John 14:27***

For Strength: *"I can do all this through him who gives me strength."* ***Philippians 4:13***

For Encouragement: *"Be strong and courageous… for the Lord your God will be with you wherever you go."* ***Joshua 1:9***

For Guidance: *"Trust in the LORD with all your heart, and do not lean on your own understanding. In all your ways acknowledge Him, and He will make straight your paths."* ***Proverbs 3:5-6***

For Bravery: *"So do not fear, for I am with you; do not be dismayed, for I am your God. I will strengthen you and help you; I will uphold you with my righteous right hand."* ***Isaiah 41:10***

For Confidence: *"For the Spirit God gave us does not make us timid, but gives us power, love and self-discipline."* ***2 Timothy 1:7***

For Motivation: *"Let us not become weary in doing good, for at the proper time we will reap a harvest if we do not give up."* ***Galatians 6:9***

For Comfort: *"The God of all comfort… comforts us in all our troubles, so that we can comfort those in any trouble…"* ***2 Corinthians 1:3-4***

For Courage: *"The Lord is my light and my salvation—whom shall I fear?"* ***Psalm 27:1***

For Gratitude: *"Enter his gates with thanksgiving and his courts with praise; give thanks to him and praise his name."* **Psalm 100:4**

For Uncertainty: *"So do not worry, saying, 'What shall we eat?' or 'What shall we drink?' or 'What shall we wear?' For the pagans run after all these things, and your heavenly Father knows that you need them. But seek first His kingdom and His righteousness, and all these things will be given to you as well. Therefore do not worry about tomorrow, for tomorrow will worry about itself. Each day has enough trouble of its own."* **Matthew 6:31–34**

Bonus Scriptures

When I feel the need to lean on God's love and support more than usual, I remember and read these scriptures that keep my spirits high and my chin up.

- **Have I not commanded you? Be strong and courageous. Do not be frightened. And do not be dismayed. For the Lord, your God, is with you—wherever you go.**—*Joshua 1:9*

There is something so comforting and reassuring in times of uncertainty when you know God is always with you, wherever you go. If something makes my soul troubled, I find a reprieve by leaning on Him and finding a reprieve.

- **"He will wipe away every tear from their eyes. And death shall be no more. Neither shall there be mourning, nor crying, nor pain anymore. For the former things have passed away." And He who was seated on the throne said, "Behold, I am making all things new."**—*Revelation 21:4*

You will be open to all of the rewards of the present and all the opportunities of the future. How? By releasing the reins of the past.

Sometimes just making all things new and having that fresh start are all you need. Just focus on the unprecedented opportunities that lie ahead.

I want to emphasize that you can choose your own scriptures that you connect with the most. Whatever works for you is the right way to go about it. Whatever keeps you inspired, gives you strength and calms your mind.

Write your own inspirational quotes too if you want. Whatever will be reminders of practice that calm your mind and allow you to focus on a positive thought.

God comes in mysterious ways and takes a myriad of forms.

Always remember … you are not alone. You are not meant to live this life on your own. God lives in you. This will never change.

"Be strong and courageous. Do not be afraid or terrified… for the Lord your God goes with you; he will never leave you nor forsake you."

—Deuteronomy 31:6

CHAPTER

9

Visualization on Steroids

Since the beginning of this book, I have been emphasizing how your brain and your subconscious can work in symphony to create the future you are yearning for. I could quote a horde of scientific research (and I may still do that) to support that visualization can and does change not only brain activity but physical performance in your body.[1] However, what I am about to do is tell you how visualization changed my life, the life of a daughter, mother, sister, wife, leader, and entrepreneur.

The power of visualization is real; everyone has access to it; anyone can practice it. Visualization, to me, is how you rewire and train your brain to search for what can go right, *not* what can go wrong. Finding the bright spots and transforming that knowledge into a mental image of what you want can produce

---

[1] Meditation: In Depth | NCCIH (nih.gov).

amazing results. It has been proven to work in a variety of fields, including helping people with depression, anxiety, PTSD, chronic pain and inflammation, sports performance, professional performance under pressure, stress reduction, weight loss, and many, many more.

As I previously mentioned, I have personally experienced the power of visualization in my life. I learned how to live a life with intention and raise my standards and how to live life ... on my terms. That is when things started to change for me. The power of visualization was the icing on the cake to call my desires into existence. You can want change in your life; but if you don't know what that change looks like, you'll be like a hamster on a wheel, running yet staying in the same place, which is why visualization is a vital ingredient to changing your life.

How did I do that? Let me tell you ...

Can You See Your Target?

We previously explored the concept that all aspects of life possess energy. By intentionally directing this energy, you can shape your reality to conquer goals. Manifesting your desired outcomes requires consistent daily actions that have the additional benefit of boosting your confidence and expanding the possibilities you perceive for yourself and your circumstances.

We talked about the fight-or-flight instinct we all possess, what protects us from what can unexpectedly go wrong. By implementing the opposite of that approach, you can visualize an image in your mind's eye, where even the smallest detail describes exactly what can go right *(aka, what you want to happen)*.

Take a moment and remember a particular situation that comes to mind in great detail. For example, imagine last night, you were sitting on the couch, watching a movie, eating popcorn, and drinking a glass of OJ. Think a bit harder. Can you

Visualization on Steroids

remember the taste of the fresh juice, cold and tangy, touching your tongue? The smell of that popcorn? Can you remember the softness of the couch? Were you comfortable or uncomfortable? Did you have a pillow behind your back?

It's like you are right there again, right?

Now ... with the same visualization intensity as before, using as many of your five senses (visual, auditory, olfactory, kinesthetic and gustatory) as possible, build in your mind something you want to happen in your life. Maybe you have a customer meeting, but you are worried about the consequential response of asking for what it is you want.

Sit down; close your eyes (or not; whatever feels more comfortable for you), continuing to use your visualization intensity to build the image of you—asking for their business. See yourself walking through that door, making that handshake (feel the handshake) ... Smelling the leather on the chair where you will sit ... See yourself doing your presentation to influence the sale ... Imagine the taste of water you are sipping during the conversation ... Hear the words coming from your customer expressing gratitude of how insightful your presentation was ... Seeing their facial expression—and approving the deal. Feel the feeling in your stomach when that happens—the relief, the joy ... the excitement ... the call you are making to your best friend that you got the sale where you're smiling from ear to ear.

This is how visualization works. This is the power of your mind.

Visualizing yourself successfully engaging in your goal activity is crucial to jumpstarting the rest of your life forward. It's that straightforward. What better way to achieve this than by directly experiencing it first-hand? Scientific evidence has already proven that success occurs in two phases: We first envision our desired activity in our minds; this is the initial mental rehearsal phase, and then we translate those mental rehearsals into physical reality. Celebrated author Napoleon Hill eloquently sums it up in his classic book, *Think and Grow Rich*, "Whatever the mind can conceive and believe, it can achieve!" My modern take? "Seeing is believing," and "believing allows you to see"!

Visualization is nothing more than seeing and constructing the outcome *you* want. Plain and simple. I remember when I first moved to Connecticut, I got my real estate license and hit the ground running. I was not from Connecticut, so I knew no one. I would go to homeowners to get listings, and I would always fast-forward to the end of that appointment ... before it happened. I imagined calling my husband with such excitement. I felt it in my stomach as if it was happening. I heard his excitement, too, congratulating me. I visualized the contract being signed. Does it mean every time you go for the win, you'll land it each and every time, without fail? No, but let me tell you, it sure as heck becomes more fun. Because I am living life with full intention, I get way more wins than losses.

I clearly visualized what it is that I wanted, down to the point where I could vividly see in my mind what those things are. The sensation I felt in my stomach as if it already happened, I would intensify the feeling, using music (*eye of the Tiger* was my trigger), it got me pumped! This is the power of the subconscious mind. You have to tell it exactly what you want to get exactly what you desire. Period! When you have no mental picture, there is no intention behind the words you feed your mind. And when you focus on what you want coupled with the feelings of your five senses (or even just a couple), you create the energy required that emits a vibrational frequency, which we talked about in earlier chapters. Everything is energy. When you learn how to manipulate energy, you can have just about anything you want.

Why is this? Because it creates a neurological response in your brain to the images you put there. Just think about it, seeing images, objects, whether in your mind or in the outer world, changes the way you feel. When you see something that excites you, you will feel excited. If you see something that makes you sad, you will feel sad.

And the interesting part? You are already doing this. You are already visualizing on autopilot, which is why bringing intention to this is vital. Otherwise, you'll likely get results dictated by external circumstances.

Here are other small yet significant real examples: You say, "I have to go get bananas and milk from the store." You see yourself getting in the car, walking into the store, and you know exactly where the bananas are before you get there. You see yourself checking out and bringing them home.

You say, "I am flying to Chicago next month." You are already visualizing the airport. Some of you might start to wonder (visualize) worst-case scenarios ... will the flight be delayed since I'm flying in the middle of winter when winter storms are a higher probability; will you miss your connection; maybe the plane's cabin will be hot and musty. Remember, you haven't even left your living room yet, and you are building an image (focusing on) on all the what-ifs that on all the what-ifs that can occur!

A lot of the visualization you are currently doing is involuntary, happening so fast and unfocused, where you don't realize it. This is why it's important to recognize and take control of it. More often than not, people permit their anxiety to control their mental image of what will happen instead of the opposite—mental imagery to control anxiety.

- "What if I miss my plane?"
- "What if I don't get the promotion?"
- "What if there is a long line at the store?"
- "What if my new business idea fails?"
- "What if my children won't sit still at the restaurant?"
- "What if they don't sign the contract?"

Answer honestly. Are you on autopilot, or are you in the captain's seat of your visualization?

Focusing for a brief period of time, say three seconds, is still focusing on an image that impacts your mind and neurology. If you have the image in your mind, you give it life. Your focus activates that picture. Don't underestimate the power of that three-second thought. But there's hope. You are not doomed if you counteract it with another thought that focuses on the outcome you actually want. But if you don't take care of that negative thought, no matter how small, it can take root and grow.

Change the channel is not about living in fear that a so-called bad or negative thought or image in your mind will occur. This will happen; it happens to everyone. Sometimes they try to tell you something. This is a part of life. But when you know it is debilitating for you, then you have the power to interrupt it. Again, as we discussed, a resilient mind, one exercising grit, is what's required to get past these life's hiccups.

Change the channel is the knowledge that you have the power to replace those images with the ones you want, with the happy, positive, productive ones. Take note—Awareness alone isn't enough. It's up to you to take command, without this, your thoughts control you. You have the remote to "change the channel"! You need to be proactive, especially when negativity abounds, converging in from all sides—toward you. You need to shrink the bad picture and change the channel to something that makes you feel good. See yourself where you want to be, and the neurons in your brain will create the right response to that image. Options and solutions will make themselves known.

Think about golf. If the golf players can't visualize the ball sinking into the hole, and precisely how, they won't be able to decide what is the right club to use for the right swing. They certainly won't be able to judge the proper amount of force required to land the golf ball exactly where they want it. Any professional golfer will tell you that golf is very much a mind game. But so is everything else. Don't football and hockey also have that mental component? Name any sport or any game in life; they have one thing in common—a strong psychological element, a strong and resilient mindset.

Imagine the expertise of engineers who bring those stunning bridges to life. They have to carefully construct architectural plans, create a blueprint, and then execute it. They, too, have to see the completed bridge in their minds first before they even attempt to create the blueprint.

This process of visualization allows you to construct the very blueprint of your future, focusing your energy and intention to significantly increase the probability of achieving your deepest personal desires—without apology.

An Exercise for You

When you open your eyes tomorrow morning, (in the first few minutes) as you wake up, your brain is often in a theta or alpha state. Which means your brain is highly receptive to suggestions (affirmations) and visualization. Your subconscious mind will absorb it that much easier at this time. Avoid checking your phone immediately as the day to day distractions will intercept this creation of re-wiring your brain.. And this is the best time for you to start impregnating all that you want to manifest. This is prime time! imagine your entire day unfolding the way you want it to. Imagine where you want to go and what you want to accomplish; see yourself doing it, and … watch what happens. Cheat sheet: just go to the end of your day in advance. I promise you, you will notice a difference in how you feel. Imagine that you are at the end of your day or maybe at dinner, expressing to a loved one how great your day went. Here is the secret: when you go there in your mind, you will have experienced it already. Keep this in mind: You want to focus on what you WANT, not on what you don't want. You have to prepare your mind to search for what it needs. Give it a target. Focus on it. Visualization requires consistent practice.

The foundation you need is a mind without limits (or an imagination with no borders). Setting your intention for what you want to accomplish, perhaps before an important future event, or the perfect life partner, etc. Again, I can't state this enough ... daily practice, with your eyes open or closed. Your choice! Utilize your moments, even at bedtime, just before falling *into* sleep. Sometimes even I forget (I'm human). When things do not go as I would have liked them to, I don't even question it anymore. If I had set my intention the right way, I would have had much different results. Will it be a guaranteed success? Not necessarily, but I cannot stress this enough—the more you do it, the more wins you will have. That is what this is all about.

When you do accomplish what you had set your mind on, when the mental image you created matches reality, an excited feeling of accomplishment will warm your body. Motivation will be further engaged. And as we know, motivation is often built on previous successes. You are thus building a powerful mind-engine to take you wherever you want—all by the simple act of disciplined visualization. And visualization followed by action is what will bring that vision to life. As explained, visualization builds your belief and fuels motivation; when you couple this with action, this is what will allow you to make things happen.

Pull the trigger of your visualization and your future.

Momentum's Power Source

The RAS is a network of neurons (and one of the most important parts of your brain) located in the brain stem, where it connects with the spinal cord. This neural network operates below the

Visualization on Steroids

level of awareness, filtering all incoming and outgoing information. Specifically, RAS filters incoming information based on what it's been programmed to prioritize—via focused visualization. Essentially, it allows only relevant details to reach your conscious awareness, while ignoring what it perceives as unimportant to your current focus. These selected pieces of information are then processed into your conscious thoughts, influencing your emotions.

Imagine the moment just before you begin a painting. RAS will allow through, from the vast universe of subconscious thoughts, anything that pertains to you wanting to paint at this moment. This means all information stored in your subconscious brain about painting and the tools and skills that you have gathered pertaining to creativity. RAS is going to help you paint the masterpiece you are building in your mind.

Our brains are simply astonishing, aren't they? God created us in His image—absolute masterpieces of perfection that are supposed to work in unison with all tools available to us to lead successful and happy lives. It is up to us to get the remote and tap into the potential of this amazing, well-oiled machine.

Now think about how RAS, used in conjunction with visualization, can help you. If you keep what are your top-priority goals and build visions of them in your brain consciously, RAS will let through all the tools and supportive thoughts that are stored in your subconscious to make what your heart (and conscious mind) desires a reality. How amazing is that? It's as if you are hacking your own brain activity to access "shortcut codes" to create an advantage that will help you transform your vision into reality faster and easier.

RAS is like Google. I know you have noticed that you are searching for something on a website, and all of a sudden it shows up on your Google page, or other areas, like your social media feeds. Even creepier? You were talking to your friend about searching for an Airbnb in Hawaii, and then all of a sudden all these vacation spots start appearing on your phone. Well in a not so creepy, comparable kind of way, that is how your RAS works. So feed it like crazy, ALL that you want it to notice and to attract.

Of course, this is exactly how it works in the opposite sense, too. You have heard the saying, "When it rains, it pours," right? Why do you think that is? Well, as they say, "misery loves company." Once you get mired into that mindset, focusing, visualizing, and believing that compounding issues and problems will arise, then the more you create negative momentum.

If you are constantly worried that you are in debt, frequently counting pennies, and conjuring images in your mind of you having little to no money in the bank to pay your rent, then you have to replace those thoughts and images. Counter them with positive ones of you successfully paying your rent, of you having the money to buy abundantly what you need. The latter activates RAS, which will pull from your subconscious your archived (perhaps you might have forgotten about) resources that you can now use toward your imagery becoming a reality.

To put it in simple terms, RAS is like a genie in a bottle. You "tell it" what is important to you, what you want, and it delivers to you the tools needed to accomplish that.

When you constantly complain about your relationship, this is the image that you are building that RAS responds to, so show your subconscious what it is that you want. Visualize the self-love that you need in order to be happy, safe, and contented. And I am not talking about taking a trip to the spa to get your hair and nails done. That's not self-love; that's maintenance. Self-love is when you care about what you program into your mind, your heart, and your stomach.

BUILD THE VISION!!!

There is no better day than *today* to start doing this.

Right now, this minute, think about what it is that you desire in your heart of hearts. Create a shift in your mind that will break the cycle for you. The moment you do this, things will start happening in your life that you didn't even believe possible before.

The Power of Visualization

Oftentimes when I think about things that I have succeeded in throughout my life, *desire* is the driving force behind it all. I had an undeniable hunger for it. I encourage you to self-reflect and evaluate the level of desire you have for the life you say you want. How big is your desire, really? Would it be able to carry you to the finish line—and beyond? Visualization is a wonderful thing; it allows you to see your desires unfolding. You can feel them as if they are already happening. Imagine it being like a rehearsal to the success you want, where you become the architect of your beautiful life. But if your desire to put in the serious actions and disciplined effort is lacking, then you are wasting your time. Harsh words, I know. I only speak the truth. I'm not here to tell you what you want to hear, but what you *need to* hear. The truth might hurt at first; but in the end, it's exactly what we needed to hear in order to initiate the right change.

Are your dreams *your* dreams, or are they the dreams that society or other people around you dictate? Do you really dream of the white house with the picket fence, two kids, and a dog? Or is that what you are being told that you *should* be wanting from life?

If you naturally desire something, you will burn with the passion to accomplish it. Tapping into your subconscious potential will become effortless. You don't have to force your dreams. When you visualize what your heart wants, you feel good; you feel more confident than ever before; you will feel even happier just by simple yet touchingly beautiful thought that this is what your future holds because a dream is a vision carried out by your *desire*.

If you want to visualize that moment when you've achieved something great, or maybe your best life, think about the good feelings you've experienced. For example:

Step One

- The birth of your first child
- When you married your best friend
- When you won that game
- When you received recognition for your effort
- When you helped someone change their life
- When you graduated
- When you got the biggest deal of your career
- Your first kiss

What did this single, most proud moment feel like?

Step Two

Now recreate this feeling … with your goal in mind. Yes, right now.

Think of the moment where you felt proud.

Can you see, hear (for some include smell and taste) how it feels to make your dreams come true?

- Are you seeing in your mind's eye your loved ones? Are you smiling? Are other people around you smiling?
- What do you feel?
- What do you hear?
- What taste do you smell?
- What are you doing?

Visualization on Steroids

Do you remember your grandma's cookies? Or, if you're Latina like me, your mom's churros? Or remember that nostalgic feeling that overcomes you every time you smell cinnamon, sugar, or even hearing a tune? Using your senses to activate a powerful experiential moment is a powerful ability when properly used. You absolutely have to involve all of your senses when visualizing. You have to concentrate on sounds, images, smells, feelings, and even tastes.

I remember so vividly when I was living in Phoenix and I wanted to live in the "right part of town." I was going to Scottsdale, driving on the 101 highway and passing by the exits of the neighborhoods I wanted to live in, and I was daydreaming about how I was moving into one of the houses. I was at a stoplight, and a guy in a BMW X5 stopped next to me.

I remember looking at him and thinking, he is driving *my car*. I said it with such certainty. I didn't even think twice about it; it was the most intense feeling I had, and I couldn't explain it. All I could see was myself in this exact car ... driving it. All details were there in my mind, down to the specific feeling of holding the steering wheel. I remember seeing myself putting a CD on and listening to my favorite song. In my mind, it was a sunny day, and I vividly remember seeing myself drive off the BMW dealership parking lot. The feeling was so intense that it almost took my breath away.

Lo and behold, six months later, this exact scene played out ... in real life.

Mind you, all of this was before I realized the power of visualization. The more I thought about this feeling I got when I saw that car, the more I realized that this was why I got what I wanted. I could see it in my mind. I could smell the new leather and heard exactly what I wanted to hear. I realized that visualization was part of my success, and I started learning and pursuing that with a passion, manifesting pretty much anything I could dream of, down to the smallest detail. I started to reflect back on anything I could remember and was able to pinpoint that I did in fact see it in my mind first, before actually achieving the things that I did. Even the stuff I didn't want, I attracted it. I slowly discovered that this was no accident. When you claim it as yours, you will become it. This has happened so much that I knew it was no longer a coincidence.

Are you having that lightbulb moment when you realize you were able to attract a good or bad situation? It seems like we as humans often focus on the things that we don't want, so maybe what you are remembering now is not something you wished for but rather tried to avoid, yet with your intense focus on it you attracted it. I know, I know, hard to believe. I'm not saying that everything bad that happened to you is your fault. I have had scary things where I obsessed over it and then I came to attract it not realizing it.

Even smaller things, just like walking down the stairs with a glass of water and, in your mind's eye, seeing yourself slip and drop the water, and you tell yourself, "I hope I don't drop this," and it happens literally seconds after. That is why it is so important to visualize and speak only what it is you want to attract, the things that will move you forward. And if a thought or a word that holds you back escapes, counter it with what you want instead. Immediately! Even if you countered that with "I got this all is well."

Now, let me use a word of caution because I hear this all the time:

- "I visualized; why didn't it happen?"
- "I meditated; why can't I move forward?"

Visualization is not a magic trick. Daily practice increases your chances of accomplishing your goals, of making our dreams

Visualization on Steroids

a reality. We are working in tandem with our subconscious. But that doesn't mean nothing unforeseen or surprising will ever occur in our lives, and that we will achieve every single goal we want, thus making visualization seem like a parlor trick where we input a ticket with what we want and our subconscious spits back a prize. That's not how it works. Far from it.

When a door closes, that's for a reason. Wait for that window to open. Try something different; try to challenge why it didn't happen for you because I bet there is something even better that is waiting for you. But it will only come when you challenge it. When you pivot to the other side of rejection, which is usually where the best stuff is.

A friend recently told me a story of how she realized the power of visualization. Her dog got a routine surgery, but as soon as she picked it up from the vet, she knew there was something wrong. She couldn't explain it, but she could feel it from the dog's energy and vibration. Several days passed, and the dog showed no signs of improving; as a matter of fact, the dog's illness rapidly worsened. The doctors kept dismissing my friend, to her frustration, and she felt helpless. Then she remembered talking to me about her visualization, and she started focusing on holding her dog and visualizing the dog getting better, that he is receiving healing energy from her.

She kept doing that day and night for four straight days. The dog ended up in the ER, triggering her fear that he wouldn't last through the night. She kept praying and visualizing. Long story short, the dog survived after finding a doctor who discovered the issue (a massive internal infection that occurred during the routine surgery), and my friend was so grateful, as the dog lived many happy years after.

She told me when she finally had a conversation with the doctor who saved the dog after the ordeal ended, he told her that by every medical convention, her dog should have died.

How such a massive and deadly infection that lasted for so many days didn't kill him was beyond the doctor's imagination. This is in addition to the dog making a full recovery. But my friend knew.

That is not to say that you can heal yourself only with the power of positive thinking. Even in this example, the conventional medicine and several surgeries the dog endured are also what saved his life. However, the power of my friend's visualization helped the outcome, showering the dog with love, affection, and positive vibrations, all of that supported the whole healing process.

Remember the study I mentioned earlier about the healing process being helped by meditation? Visualize that you can help not only yourself, but also the people around you, your family, and your loved ones. The power is real and raw.

Using it and practicing this daily is what will change your life.

Just give it a shot. See it in your mind. Feel it in your heart. Take the right action. This is how you make things happen!

"Now faith is confidence in what we hope for and assurance about what we do not see."

—Hebrews 11:1

CHAPTER

10

Barriers Overrated

Have you ever caught yourself saying, "I can't do this"? When we ponder our limitations, we often focus on the barriers or obstacles hindering our progress. But in reality, is it *really* a barrier that we are talking about? Or are we making up excuses for what we are subconsciously afraid to pursue? Are we dodging the fear of disappointment? Sure, we can also come up with reasons why we can't do something:

- "I have no money to pursue my passion."
- "I have no time to work on my project."
- "I don't want to screw up."
- "I don't know what to do … (Fill in the blank)."
- "I can't do that because … (Fill in the blank)."

Sure, real-life barriers do exist. It would be irresponsible to mislead anyone otherwise. But there is always, always another way. As they say, if there is a will (and a strong will at that), there is a way!

Most obstacles that we encounter in life we place there ourselves. These self-imposed barriers—obstacles that we can actually control—often prevent us from taking the first step. Why? Because we've already convinced ourselves that the situation is *already* impossible. Remember, it all begins in your mind. *What you believe so will be.*

Even if it is not true, it will always be. If you are constantly telling yourself all the reasons why it will not work, your brain starts to treat that belief you keep repeating to yourself as truth. This repetition strengthens the surrounding neural pathways, thus creating what you experience. If you see it as possible, new pathways will form to then attract things, people, and resources that resonate with this belief. It is that simple. This universal law does not lie. If you're asking for what you want out of pure fear, then when will you finally break free from this unfulfilling cycle?

Even in business, you have to constantly ask for what you want. What do you have to lose? If anything, you increase your chances of actually getting what you want because you put that out there. Nothing irks me more in business when people don't get what they need because they allowed previous circumstances to dictate their future. For example, you have a deadline and a supplier promised you'd get it by next Wednesday, but now, your customer called and said they need it a day earlier.

You tell your customer it can't be done. What!? What!? I know, right? Never. You didn't even ask your supplier if you can get it sooner. The response is often that it is impossible, because they have never been able to turn it around earlier than three business days. So what? Ask them to. If I had a dollar, no, a penny, for every time I've seen what others perceived as impossible occur, that I was told was impossible, I would literally be able to retire my entire family two times over. By simply asking for what you want, you will see what's truly possible. It does not mean that 100% of the time it will happen, but I guarantee you more times than not, it will. People don't often challenge things because they have been sold on what external realities are. This is something I really want you to ingrain in your mind:

Ask for WHAT YOU WANT. PERIOD!

1. Ask for the project to be completed sooner. Not because you're *bossy*, but because you won't know what's possible unless you ask.
2. Ask that restaurant to make an exception when you added three more guests to your reservation last minute (oh boy I am my son's hockey team's manager go-to when she cannot get a party of 30 on a reservation).
3. Ask for that upgrade to first class.
4. Ask for health.
5. Ask for abundance.
6. Ask for a better steak!
7. Anything goes. Play with it and see what you begin to notice.

Did you ever imagine several years ago that having a worldwide shutdown was even possible? Yet, we all lived through a pandemic. Some of us endured pain from a lost loved one. Many things were uncertain, and it made planning extremely difficult. But let's say I really needed to go from A to B. Flights were canceled, and traveling was a lot more complicated. But the fact that I can't travel via air from A to B doesn't mean that I can't rent a car, or get on a train, or virtually attend my designated event.

In every situation there are many options you can explore that are within your control. Sometimes you just have to refuse to take *no* for an answer until you first *see* what else is possible. I promise you it WILL become your reality, more times than not, when you adopt a fierce "make things happen" mindset. In any awful circumstance you will never experience a better solution until you seek to see it as working out. See the better way. Then you will experience it being so, regardless of the odds; regardless of when others tell you that it can't be done.

I'm telling you from experience I have made some unbelievable things happen in my life, which most viewed impossible. I've also had the privilege of witnessing real transformation occur in the lives of the clients whom I coach. I've stretched my limits beyond belief. Because I knew that if I didn't, I would never know what was truly possible. Just go for it. If you want to go big, this is where it's at. This is what you must do to receive different results than your average person. If you feel fine with whatever results then who am I to tell you to go bigger? Most people do not stretch themselves, challenge the status quo; in fact, most will not even think it's possible because they never stretched themselves to see. Once you do, you will be next level.

What I want you to understand here is that barriers to your dreams can only exist because you chose to quit after a challenge of some kind. But the killer of dreams only occurs when you continue to believe that your skills and capabilities are limited. Or you make excuses that your present station in life is perfect; that there is no need to progress. Yet deep down you wish you did. Barriers are nothing short of opportunities for you to go again, opportunities to change what you're doing to get a different outcome.

Self-imposed excuses fortify and strengthen your barriers. Eventually they'll feel unbreakable, causing you to feel stuck.

You won't live a life that is truly fulfilling on your terms. You will perceive even the smallest setback as a gigantic roadblock that will prevent you from moving forward, thus effectively paralyzing your ability to grow.

When something bad happens in your life, do you let it stop you from living your life to the fullest? Do you wallow in pity and focus on all the things in life you will never be able to do? Or will you choose to find a different path to reach your dreams and focus on the things that are in your control? Would you even invent new possibilities to get you to where you want to be?

If, in a moment like that, you stop and ask yourself, "Could this be worse?" it will allow you to see the gravity of the situation, and expand your perspective. We often do see our problems bigger than they are. If you get a group of 100 people in a circle and tell them to place all their problems in the middle, you will realize by looking at everyone else's issues that yours aren't as bad as you thought. Your intense focus caused your problems to exponentially magnify.

There really are so many examples of people who live happy and fulfilled lives in spite of the real barriers they must encounter. So, why would you give power to your *perceived* barriers that you put in your own way? Your perspective matters. If you see everything as hard and with no possibility for improvement, guess what? That is exactly what it will be, and you will be stuck in the Land of the Impossible. You can make everything 20 times harder even when it doesn't need to be, just because your perception is that it will be difficult.

- "Oh, it won't work out …"
- "Oh, I know they'll say no …"
- "Oh, I can't figure this out …"
- "Oh, I could never …"

And so on and so forth.
So, what can you do about it?

- Change your language patterns.
- Counter your negative thoughts.
- Improve your self-talk.

Meet challenges head-on with *"Yes, this might be hard, but it doesn't matter; because I will push through and figure it out, and make it happen!"* When you put directions in Waze or Google Maps, and it encounters traffic or construction road blocks, does it tell you to turn around and go home? No, it re-routes you. Same with challenges, it's an opportunity for you to simply pivot, to grow, to think differently about how to get there. I doubt that there is someone out there who doesn't want to make things smoother or easier for themselves. You, too? Then what are you waiting for?

If you claim that you can push through it, that you can overcome it, it's not a barrier anymore. It's just a minor annoyance that you will deal with, and then promptly forget about. You just have to truly believe that you are capable of doing so. If anyone can do it, then why not you? Why not now?

This is where your faith comes in. Faith in yourself, that you are strong enough, that you are deserving and capable enough. Faith that God has your back, and that He will carry you through the hard times and bless you with His love. Faith that you will find and receive the support you need just because you are open to it and because you know it's out there.

Breaking the Chains of Guilt

Self-imposed barriers, though often unseen, can be the most challenging to overcome. One such pervasive barrier is guilt. This heavy emotional burden clouds our minds, distorts our vision of what we truly desire, and ultimately restrains us from pursuing fulfilling opportunities.

Guilt often stems from past actions—perceived failures, unspoken words, the inability to forgive past missteps, or the expanse between who we were ... and who we believed we *should* be. Whatever its origin, self-forgiveness is the route to overcoming guilt. A powerful tool for this process is to engage with our former selves. Through honest self-reflection and inner dialogue, we can confront past hurts, clear our minds, and extend forgiveness—both to ourselves and to those who have wounded us. This act of letting go allows us to grow, to move on—unburdened.

Let me be clear: the struggle with guilt is a universal human experience; and yet, to progress, we must release the grip that our past has on us and focus on the potential of who we are today and the aspirations of our future. For growth is inherent to the human experience. We naturally strive to be better than our former selves, and our future selves will undoubtedly aim for further improvement, so it is imperative to release this emotional baggage. Refusing to do so dims the positive developments in our lives, including our evolving relationships. Furthermore, opportunities right before you, or what's on the horizon, will be obscured.

Guilt serves no constructive purpose. Imagine carrying heavy chains—the weight of past regrets—as you navigate life. You may not realize that this is in fact happening, but it is. Whether rooted in past misdeeds, harsh self-criticism, or a preoccupation with potential failures attributed to past mistakes, this burden hinders your progress. It's like releasing those shackles that have been weighing heavy.

I, too, have navigated the complexities of guilt. As a working mother, I wrestled for years with the conflicting demands of career and family, feeling inadequate in both roles. If I was at home, I felt that the business was suffering; if I was working, I felt I was neglecting my kids. This "mommy guilt" created significant stress and unhappiness until I consciously chose acceptance and peace with my decisions and priorities, recognizing that I was already doing a damn good job juggling my responsibilities, which brought me immense relief. I knew that I was a good mom and that my kids know that they are my #1 priority. What I came to realize later is that part of being a good parent is showing your kids not only your work ethic and dedication but also living a life with purpose and meaning.

Therefore, I urge you to grant yourself a break. Don't be so hard on yourself. Acknowledge that you are doing great. Prioritize your own well-being. Don't postpone your own needs indefinitely, waiting for some ideal scenario. Make the time for yourself now; you are important. Embrace the principle of putting on your oxygen mask *first*, because your well-being matters. Pursue the life that ignites your passion, without feeling the need to sacrifice other important aspects of your life. Loving yourself enough to pursue your heart's desires, despite external opinions, is paramount.

My own journey into inspirational speaking was met with skepticism. Many questioned why I would add another demanding role to my already full life. Yet, this was a calling I needed to answer for myself. Despite well-intentioned warnings about the challenges, I focused on my ability to manage it all with grace and intention.

Perhaps it's human nature to be driven by doubt. The more I was told it couldn't be done, the more determined I became to prove otherwise. While I acknowledge some of the potential difficulties with juggling it all, my deep-seated calling propelled me forward. It was a passion I could no longer ignore, a gift I felt compelled to share.

Fortify Boundaries

Crucially, I established boundaries to protect my time and energy, a principle I encourage you to adopt too. By clearly defining my commitments, I ensured that my key priorities remained at the forefront. I strive to practice what I preach, sharing lessons born from my triumphs and tribulations, my lived experience. This is why I emphasize the vital importance of making time for what matters most in your life.

The positive impact my work has on others is deeply rewarding. However, I recognize that my own sustained happiness depends on maintaining equilibrium. Setting boundaries dictates how much of myself I can authentically share with the world.

My passion lies in empowering those who seek more from life. Yet, to sustain this work, I must prioritize my own well-being. This is not a sprint; it's a marathon. My vision extends toward a future where, as a content and fulfilled 95-year-old and beyond, I am still learning and helping others, guided by a deep understanding of the human mind. This vision is one free from the burden of guilt, knowing I honored my boundaries and protected my capacity to give.

Guilt-Free Living Is the Key

But what if your unique gift to the world hasn't yet emerged? That is a perfectly legitimate question to ask. Releasing guilt paves the way for forgiveness both of self and of others who have hurt or disappointed you, regardless of the severity. You break free from the shackles of the past, allowing your passions and calling to rise to surface of your consciousness. Trust that the universe responds to openness and faith. And now that you are open, you will start to receive more of what you want because you've released the energy of holding good to enter into your life. You are now vibrating a new frequency, one where you're ready to receive.

Resist the temptation to force discovery. Your purpose will reveal itself; it will be an extraordinary revelation. When it does, embrace it—fiercely! Embarking on the journey toward your envisioned life requires courage and a willingness to shed the weight of the past.

Remember ... live guilt-free!

When Fear Comes Knocking

You are probably wondering why I say WHEN fear knocks on your door. As I said before, fear is a natural part of life; therefore, I believe it's not a matter of IF but a matter of WHEN you will encounter it. And believe me, I am the most optimistic human being on the planet, but we have covered the fight-or-flight response throughout this book, and I cannot pretend that it doesn't happen.

Ruminating thoughts such as: *"What if they tell me no?" "What if I get bad news after my doctor's appointment?"* or *"What if I am not good enough?"* can rob you of your peace, disturb your equilibrium, and prolong your journey to fulfill your goals and dreams.

Why? Because we are creatures of manifestation. What I am talking about is not the physical signs of being scared or experiencing fear symptoms, if you will. You can potentially manifest something far worse than what was thought possible if your negative thinking continues to interfere. And no, I am not talking about the fearful thoughts that are meant to evoke change to look within on what these fearful thoughts are telling you. Sometimes

Barriers Overrated

they are flat out innocent, like, what if I forget my keys? They are there to help you plan and anticipate future potential roadblocks; however, recognize when they are to your determinant.

This is exactly where "change the channel" comes into play. It has been so inspiring to see how this simple yet powerful concept I came up with two decades ago has helped so many people move past moments of private fears and frustrations toward peace.

Remember, we are a vibration of what we exude, knowing that we have 100% control over whether or not you choose to answer the call of F.E.A.R. ...when it comes knocking.

Or you can slam the door in the face of fear and choose to open another door that leads to a place of hope, peace, and opportunity. When you do that, life begins to happen *for* you instead of *to* you. You allow hope to guide you versus fear. You'll discover that your feelings will energetically flow easier toward the direction of your purposeful intention. An air of lightness will envelop you. This is when you are thriving, shattering every glass ceiling you can think of! You are successful and powerful, and attractive, and desired, because of YOU and who YOU are, and what you are capable of.

Get that YES for your project. Get the news from your doctor that you are healthy and strong. See yourself feeling powerful and worthy of love and happiness and adventure. See yourself proving them all wrong. That will change how you feel and the vibration that you emit.

I don't want to hear, "Easy for you to say all of this when you don't have to deal with bad news." I know that. I have been there. If it was easy, we wouldn't need to practice changing the channel all the time. I, too, have been faced with fear. One too many times, actually.

When a self-sabotaging thought comes, creating fear or the wrong what-ifs, I choose in that moment to change the channel to one that was encouraging, a hopeful one, and tuned to gratitude. Gratitude and fear cannot simultaneously occupy the same time-space context. Try it. You'll see. It is impossible. Gratitude wins—every time. Remember when I said earlier that what you are focusing on will determine how you feel? Being mindful of this is huge. This bears repeating ... It is not about bad things happening at all. It is about you not keeping them alive. Don't make the fire bigger than it has to be. You are always being driven by one of two places, faith or fear. One moves you forward while the other one holds you back. You get to choose. Now, let me ask you: Which one will you choose the next time?

As I awaited my test results, I closed my eyes and saw myself in my mind being incredibly grateful to God for helping me to stay resolute. I got the support I needed from Him. He had my back, and I knew He would walk hand in hand with me, whatever happens. I felt peace.

Trust me; it is a hard thing to pull off in the heat of the moment. That's why you need to practice changing the channel as if your life depends on it. I am saying this because, more often than not, the life you want, the life you dream of, really does depend on it. Change the channel at every opportunity, until it becomes muscle memory.

You cannot have peace if you live in fear. No matter what happens, there is something better for you on the other side of fear. Think about that every time when you decide upfront if you will have a good or bad day, or if whatever you are to embark on will be easy or hard. Make the change; make the switch to the right channel, the channel that will have you victoriously leap into the air.

I started showing my kids the power of not only our words, but the intention of what they wanted their day to be. It is our ritual. I started doing this many years ago. When it's my turn to drive them to school, we talk about what each of us is grateful for, and then we end with what our intention is for the day. My kids at first would not take it too seriously. My boys would say, "Have a fun day." Or "Have fun at recess." While all good intentions, I wanted to get them to think deeper. So every day was not the same thing. The oldest of my two younger boys said to me, "Have a great day," which was great to hear. However, what I did not realize was what he shared with me after doing this for a few months. He said, "Mommy, you know how I said I was going to have the best day ever? It really was the best day ever, I couldn't believe it."

Truth is, he kept saying he would have a "fun day" or a "great day" and while he said this deep down he didn't really necessarily believe it. He just went along with this exercise mommy asked him to do. So the lesson here? The MORE YOU REPEAT the things you want to experience, you will become it. He said it so much that it even surprised him!

I don't want F.E.A.R. for myself and my family. That is why I am obsessed with researching 100-year-old influencers during their time and their stories. There is so much they have in common in the way they perceive the world. For example, they all confirmed what I already truly believe … that stress and worry have no place in your life. As one of these influencers shared, *"I don't worry about anything because it all works out in the end. Always!"* And I believe that it does. If you ask anyone in their 90s what is the #1 piece of advice you would give to your younger self, 90% of the time, you hear, *"I wish I would have worried less."*

I often think about this, and I have developed a strategy for myself to deal with uncertainty and fear. Every time when I begin to worry, I go to my 95-year-old self and ask, *"What would that Diana tell me about my situation?"* And I listen. I know that when I am 95 years old, I will have a lot of crazy stories to tell; I will have a lot more wisdom and experience. But most of all, I will still have the burning desire to keep learning and growing even beyond 95.

Now, imagine what your 95-year-old self would tell you!? Let that sink in for a minute.

Just asking this question of your future self is powerful. Then, sit in silence, ready to receive the answer. Whether it is to worry less, forgive more, laugh more, have more fun, or take more risks, it doesn't matter. You'll know which answer is meant for you for this particular moment in time!

Take that advice and run with it! I know that when we talk about fear, we often focus on the feeling. The point is *not* to fear ... but the *feeling* of fear itself. The thing that you should consider is the self-sabotage that fear breeds. We have a lot more power to ruin ourselves than any negative circumstance ever can. Let that sink in. You hold the control to change the channel in your life. It is your choice. You can be your worst enemy. Or you can tap the greatest asset that our God has given you.

- What would you do?
- What would you choose?
- Where will you go from here on?

It is up to you.

Just remember, when fear knocks on your door, you don't have to entertain unwelcome guests.

"So do not fear, for I am with you; do not be dismayed, for I am your God. I will strengthen you and help you; I will uphold you with my righteous right hand."

—*Isaiah 41:10*

CHAPTER

11

Create a Life Worth Living

Asking yourself powerful questions may seem hard to remember. Yet another thing out of the 37 that you have to remember. Out of all the things in your life, this definitely has to be primary because it is life changing. I shared with you how I got pushed forward by my unsettled mind, a young 26-year-old, who kept thinking to herself, this cannot be the rest of my life. Many years passed after that, but the passion for sharing my knowledge was born that night out of that question. At that time, I knew there had to be something more than living a mediocre life, settling. But having experienced it and lived it is why I knew I had to share it.

That night I asked myself the hard, life-changing questions that brought me to where I am today. The questions YOU ask yourself to build your future. I see others often settling for less than their heart desires. I wrote this book because I was one of them. I was the one wondering, "How can I live a life of real purpose and live life on my terms? How can I stop settling and have more? How?"

Today I have the answer, with certainty—by creating it for yourself. I knew that in the end, I will set aside time to talk to you, yes YOU, the person reading this book, that this magic of magical living on your terms is what I keep talking about, the life that you are ready to live, it relies on three things in terms of how you show up. What you feed your mind, heart, and your second brain, your stomach.

Leverage on Gratitude

I talk about gratitude throughout this book. I don't believe we can talk about gratitude enough.

In a recent study[1] about gratitude and how it improves the mental health of psychotherapy clients, scientists discovered the profound impact gratitude has on our brains and our ability to live happy and fulfilling lives. There are many studies that have explored that topic with people who were already happy and content, but in the aforementioned study, the participants were individuals who were already struggling with mental health issues like depression, stress, and anxiety.

The results were even more impressive, as the overall health and well-being of the people who practiced daily gratitude had improved at a much more rapid rate, and the brain changes showed on MRI scans way after the gratitude practice was complete.

---

[1] Joel Wong, Y., Owen, J., Gabana, N.T. et al. (2018). Does gratitude writing improve the mental health of psychotherapy clients? Evidence from a randomized controlled trial. *Psychotherapy Research* 28 (2): 192–202. https://doi.org/10.1080/10503307.2016.1169332.

What does that tell us? It tells us that gratitude is one of the most important daily practices you have to set aside time for. It works on so many levels, and it can truly change your life. Not only that, but you will notice even better results with consistency over time. It will change your life in so many ways.

I say this all the time, but it is true—you cannot be fearful and doubtful and be in a grateful state at the same time. Try it if you don't believe me. If your anxiety and stress levels are high, if you are feeling depressed and tired, try writing, saying, or simply thinking statements of gratitude toward anything and anyone in your life.

When you are thinking about all the things and people you are grateful for in your life, you tap into a powerful resource. When things go wrong, as they sometimes will, you will feel tested, you will feel frustrated, or angry, and at that moment, you have to learn to stop, take a deep breath, and think about everything you are grateful for. Don't question it or wonder how this practice changes everything; just do it, and watch the difference!

What Can You Be Grateful For?

Honestly, anything and everything. It can be as simple as being able to open your eyes in the morning. It can be gratitude for your healthcare team that will make you whole. It can be something related to the people around you, the people who support and love you. It can be about the everyday things that we take for granted—clean water, food on the table, a roof over your head.

It can be about that meticulously planned family vacation that you have been waiting for. It can be for professional success in your job, recognition, or just simply a successful completion of a project. It can be a personal high about your parenting skills—having my boys jump in the shower on time at bedtime without me repeating myself eight times is a cause for celebration!

When I say you can have gratitude for anything, I mean it. You know in your heart what you feel grateful for. Sometimes you could be grateful that a particular situation isn't as bad as it could be. Just BE GRATEFUL. Feel it with all your heart and soul. Make it a part of your daily routine, until it becomes a habit. Gratitude always wins.

Going to sleep with gratitude and waking up with gratitude is the best feeling. Even if you are tired during the day, be grateful for the energy you do have, as some people are not as privileged. Gratitude is something that is always there for you; it will help you to feel calmer and improve your mental health and well-being.

You can practice it anywhere.

- You are waiting in line at the grocery store? Practice gratitude.
- You are sitting at your desk in between meetings? Practice gratitude.
- You are having a rough time? Practice gratitude.
- You just got a win? Practice gratitude.

Are you having an amazing time? Practice gratitude. And the best part? You can also cultivate better habits by involving your kids or anyone around you.

I do a fun exercise with my boys. We do "Gratitude Grapes." I have been teaching them from a very young age the importance of gratitude; and if I forget, they make sure to remind me when we need to practice. Gratitude Grapes is a game I created to make gratitude practice fun for the little ones, something that they can relate to.

Create a Life Worth Living

I started by putting a blanket on the floor and we pretend we are having a picnic (in our living room if it's too cold outside, they love it!). We get a bowl of grapes, and the bowl goes around with everyone picking a grape, eating it, and sharing what they are grateful for. The energy it creates in the family is amazing. We feed off of each other's gratitude and the sense of calmness and love, especially just before going to bed in the evening.

This exercise works wonders with highly energetic children, as the state of gratitude induces a calm and relaxed state. The results are astounding. Everyone absolutely loves our family practice. I am always so amazed by the wonderful and sweet things my young boys are grateful for, and it warms my heart that they are sharing them with my husband and me. They are grateful for simple things, not big audacious or materialistic things.

They are grateful for the trees that produce oxygen and the air we breathe today. They are grateful to cuddle with mommy before bed. They are grateful for the opportunity to go to school. My favorite is when they say they are grateful for God. Teaching your kids about God is the greatest gift you can give to them as well as teach them. Having faith that God sees and is readily available to them is what will get them through life, more than you know. In all the moments, God is there—living *in* them.

We have so much to learn from the innocence of children. We often lose that as grown-ups, and it is hard to focus our gratitude on the simple, more ordinary things that we take for granted. In order to create a life worth living, it's important to be grateful for what you have now, no matter where you are. Don't knock your current situation.

If you want to create the life you want, you have to be able to step on to something to raise yourself up. That something is *your current life, your current situation*. Your future needs something to grasp onto in order for it to grow even bigger than your dreams. When you dismiss what you do have now, there is nothing to grasp onto.

When you are too busy complaining about your current life, about what you have now, you are placing your focus on the wrong things. You have to fall in love with your journey and where you are now to be able to appreciate and achieve where you want to go next. Otherwise, you will never be happy. Remember, happiness is not a destination. Gratitude should be part of your DNA.

Authenticity Matters

In our lives we often wear a mask, a facade if you will, of who we think we are supposed to be. Whether or not it is society's expectation or our family, or we are forcing these expectations on ourselves; oh, the burden! Be a great mom, great partner, show up to all the kids' activities even when you're barely breathing. Trying to look perfect with your outgrown hair or nails because you missed your appointment; oh, and for you women, your smudged mascara, looking like a raccoon. All while trying to find time for yourself and discover your purpose.

We all know what the pressure to be perfect feels like. Enough trying to prove that you're a good person. That you're attractive enough. That you're good enough.

We all are supposed to have it all, at *all* times; if we are not perfect enough, then there is something wrong with us. This unfair societal pressure has driven women and men to wear a facade, hiding their true selves. We are literally walking insecurities on high heels at times, aren't we?! Our poor husbands. For you men, you can feel this too.

I have been there, done that. But let me tell you, when you can really be yourself and be comfortable in your own skin, no matter the audience, it is absolutely liberating. We are talking in this book a lot about your goals, your passion, and your purpose. In order for you to become who you are meant to be, you have to show up in the light with who you are and be okay with all your imperfections. We get so caught up on other people's opinions that it paralyzes us from living our true authentic self. Enough of the "I got it all put together" facade. We think if we just worry hard enough then the problems disappear. They don't. Let's do better, right now. Today.

Being authentic is a prerequisite for happiness. When you realize that you are a good person, deserving praise and admiration for where you are and what you've accomplished, no matter how big or small it seems, you will be able to appreciate and love yourself even more. And yes, even with your "imperfections" and mistakes you've made. We talked about forgiving yourself so you can release those shackles, which in turn will help you become the person you want to be much, much easier.

You should never have another human being or external factors hold the keys to the kingdom of who you are and what you are worth. You are special for what you bring to the table, in any relationship, career, and endeavor you wish to pursue.

When you aren't embracing your authentic self, you are going to attract circumstances, people, and situations that are not genuine as well. You should always be unapologetically yourself because that is who the people around you will appreciate and fall in love with. Maybe that person is not as well put together as you want, but so what? People want to interact with the real you.

If you are looking for a genuine soul to match yours, a real companion who will make your heart sing, then you, too, need to be genuine and authentic.

Real people lose their temper. Real people cry. Truth is we are all a work in progress. It's never about being perfect 24/7/365.

It's the journey of what and who you strive to be. Through the thick of success and disappointments. You are deserving of compassion.

What matters is what you do every day to get better. Where even your kids or loved ones can see you apologize because of how you reacted while feeling stressed. Let them see you as you are with all your imperfections and when they see you apologize for your mistakes, you are teaching them that it's not about being perfect but recognizing your wrongdoings and owning them. Making it right.

Start eliminating your insecurities today, right now. You will see how you will blossom into a beautiful butterfly who is unafraid to get out of the cocoon and show the world the beauties of your imperfections. You need to let go of your past mistakes to allow yourself to flourish. Shed what you went through, what debilitates you, what makes you feel insecure or unworthy! You don't need to pretend you are someone you are not.

If you are genuinely unhappy with who you are, I challenge you to have an internal dialog with yourself. Go deep within to do the work internally. You will be amazed at what you'll discover that you have been perhaps avoiding the hard truth you will face. That's when you will be liberated from judgment on yourself. Where you will become your biggest fan and influence yourself to feel how deserving of happiness you are. I can write a book specifically for you that tells you how great you are, how unique you are, and how deserving of happiness you are, but if you truly don't believe that in your heart of hearts, then nothing will change. Do you believe you are deserving of happiness? If you don't, how are you going to show up in an authentic way for the people in your life?

Ask yourself the hard question—what is holding me back from being myself?

Are you putting too much weight on other people's opinions? Do you believe that you have nothing to show yet? Or maybe you had a bad experience that made you think that putting up a facade is the better option. But when you embark on a new relationship, and you are trying to build a partnership of trust and love, the most beautiful way to do that is to be open and honest, with all your cards on the table.

I remember dating as a single mom and all the experiences I had because I wasn't ready to commit to anyone. I did not want a serious "let's settle down" relationship, and that is why I did not attract one. I was scared to commit. I wanted to be free to leave anytime I felt a twinge that my relationship was getting too serious. I didn't want to be in a situation where I felt dependent on a relationship. My past experience made me wary of anything that could limit my freedom of choice or movement, and being connected to another human being on such a deep level was just not something I was interested in at that point in my life.

And then, I sat down and had a long conversation with my inner future self, and I decided that enough was enough. I was tired of games, and I wanted to attract a person who would be in my life and appreciate me for who I truly am; a person who will take me as I am, with all my craziness, feisty personality, and wit. A person who will also cherish my big heart and appreciate that I would give anyone the world if I could. I opened up my heart, raised my standards, and I said to myself that the next person I am going to date will be my husband.

When I met my husband, there were no games. It was all honesty. We were both very genuine and open in our conversations and expectations. And at that moment, I knew that this man was exactly who was meant for me. He took me for my authentic value. He looked at my flaws, and he adored them. He looked at my faults, and they didn't scare him. And I did the same for him. That is how a true partnership is built.

Don't get me wrong; I understand that sometimes in life there are circumstances that prevent you from being yourself simply because you want to protect yourself and the people you love. But you have to figure out how to break free from that. You have to have the courage to open the door to your true self and to know it won't break you.

What are you afraid of, that people won't see your beauty and the "baggage" you bring? That is not something YOU need to concern yourself with. That is their problem, not yours. If you truly love yourself, it doesn't matter what you have; it matters who you are. Same with the past, it doesn't matter what you have done in the past; it matters who you choose to be today, right now. It matters what actions you will take to be your authentic self and how you will accomplish your goals to build the life that you truly want.

Grow that unconditional love for yourself. Be proud of your scars. Know your worth. Because when you go inside and work on you, the rest will come. This is exactly what happened to me.

Create Life on Your Terms

I know that what we are talking about in this chapter might seem inconceivable, but it is true—you can have whatever life you want to have, a life on your own terms. I know you are ready to open your mind, your heart, and your arms to welcome that new life that you are dreaming of.

Have you ever thought about what that life would be like for you? Does it look like working three jobs to pay the bills? Does it look like being stressed and juggling a million things while constantly feeling you have failed in the expectation of you being the perfect parent, perfect partner, perfect professional? Are you chasing the next thing, hoping the achievement will satisfy you? I sure hope not.

Have you considered what it is that you want to do or who you want to become? Can you see yourself living life without barriers of money, or health, or any type of obstacle? Forget about what money you need for what you want to accomplish. Imagine what would your best life look like?

Start painting the picture of what you want. Picture yourself in it. What is it that your heart desires? In order to achieve anything in life, you need to know what that achievement looks like. Remember when we talked about the Reticular Activating System (RAS)? You have to know where you are going in order to be able to get there. Give your brain that target. Because if you don't know where you want to go, you will end up going somewhere else.

You can "have it all" on your own terms. You can meet your life partner; you can retire at whatever age you dream of, you can earn your coveted degree, you can get that promotion, you can build that business that is meaningful …

WHAT IS IT THAT YOU WANT?

What are you willing to do to get there? You are not meant to live a mediocre life, but you still need to put in the effort to build your life the way you want it to be, on your own terms. You can have more, and you can create more in your life. And in order to do that, you have to learn how to "change the channel" on the things that are occupying space that do not serve you. You need to start saying no to the things and people who are not growing you and recognize and say yes to the opportunities and people who support and grow you.

When I told you about my barriers to speaking engagements, I was saying no to the events that I felt would take me away from what is the most important thing in my life—my family. Although I love what I do, even the things you are the most passionate about require boundaries. I love the fact that now I feel comfortable with who I am, where I come from, and where I am now. That I can say no to the things that do not align with my priorities in any season, my family. I feel unapologetically proud of the future I'm building and the confidence to boldly pursue it.

Take a hard look at where you are now. What are you doing? What is it doing for you? Are you building the life of your dreams? Or are you just surviving?

Are your true aspirations on the back burner?

There is no reason you cannot have the life you desire. When you picture it you will feel it. You need to have it burned into your mind's eye to the point you will feel you can touch it. What did we talk about earlier in the book? In order to receive, you have to ask. Living life on your terms means you have the guts and sometimes the audacity to ask for what it is that you really, truly, deeply want.

When we grow up, we are often discouraged from asking for what we want. In some cultures, it is even considered rude to ask for what you want. How often do we say to our kids, "You get what you get, and you don't get upset"? But why? Why are we not teaching them from a young age that they should absolutely ask for what they want? They should absolutely work toward getting it. In reality, however, if you do not ask for what you want, you will still receive something, but it won't be what you want or what you need to live life on your terms.

And yes, I do understand that there is a difference between an unreasonably screaming toddler and a grown adult. But I also truly believe that this pretend satisfaction is not serving our children in the long run. We need to explain (granted not to the toddler because those little monsters are beyond any reasoning yet) that if they truly want something, there is no reason for them not to apply everything in their possession—drive, knowledge, talents, opportunities, skills, perseverance—to get it.

And this is truly living on your own terms. It's not about you receiving something you don't deserve for free. It requires effort; it requires dedication; it requires strength and guts. But you can absolutely get it. You can absolutely achieve it, and you should never ever tell them, and yourself, that it is impossible.

Remember: IMPOSSIBLE = *I'M POSSIBLE*

This is the power of the true, authentic you. Don't ask out of fear. Ask with a hopeful heart, letting the hope of your heart's desire lead the way.

Build the image of your life on your own terms. Many people (including myself) use vision boards. I talked about this earlier in the book. It will help you visualize the life you truly desire, do it. Create your heart's utmost desire in images and color them in possibility. Vision boards are a phenomenal way to build the mental image of what you are going for. It is actually one of the things I am truly proud of for bringing to our team every year.

Every year we do a company-wide contest with vision boards built with the goals of each department. It is a transformational experience, especially for those who have not used vision boards before. The energy that we exude, the power of that vibration we create with this simple but creative exercise, is like an avalanche—it engulfs everything and everyone present, and there is no denying the power of it. And the best part? You can do this with anyone of any age. My husband and I do it with our kids, and we have a fun time building the visions of the future they desire. I love seeing their creativity and excitement while they create their own boards together.

You can do it too! Stop thinking if you can achieve the best life you want. Stop thinking about "what's realistic." Focus on it. Adjust your lens and see it—clearly. It will be as realistic as your vision is.

You are never lost; you just need clarity.

- What does it look like?
- What would you be able to do if you achieved your best life?
- What is the reason you want it to look like this?

Below is an exercise I want to challenge you to do to *Create a Life Worth Living*.

1. Think about what it is you would like to accomplish. It can be anything, small or big.
2. Write out your goal. You can even write out two to three goals. Dare to dream big! It takes the same energy to pursue a big goal as it does a small one.
3. Write out the purpose of why. Why do you want this goal? What about this goal excites you?
4. Visualize it as if it has already happened. Imagine it as if you have zero limitations. Who's with you? What are you achieving? What will you now be able to do as a result of having achieved this?
5. For each goal, list three steps that you will take, every day or every week, toward that goal. It can be anything. Even writing a chapter for your book or doing research. Or asking better questions.
6. Feed your mind. Spend even 5 minutes a day in your gratitude journal.
7. Celebrate the journey! Weekly or monthly, review your progress, celebrate wins, and adjust as needed.

"For I know the plans I have for you," declares the Lord, "plans to prosper you and not to harm you, plans to give you hope and a future."

—*Jeremiah 29:11*

CHAPTER

12

Be Open to Receive ... More

We have talked about the importance of having the right mindset, of loving yourself, of asking for what you want to receive, and all of these are important parts of your journey to a better life. However, no matter what you do, if you are not open to receiving more, then the life you yearn for will continue to sit on the sidelines and have no chance to take flight.

What does it mean to be open to receive more? Opening your heart, your mind, and your soul to receive more is like opening an actual door to let the new, good energy in. Just like in springtime cleaning, you open the windows, you let the fresh air in, you clean all the exposed and not that exposed surfaces in your house of any speck of dust and dirt, and you are welcoming the new season. Welcoming the new season in your life is quite the same.

You know the saying, "if you build it, they will come"? When your entire being is open to new opportunities, new possibilities, new thoughts, new emotions, new habits, new connections ... all of that will come. You can't be open and incessantly complaining about what is wrong in your life, about how bad your current situation is, or how miserable you feel. When you focus on that, you are not allowing for something different to show up at your door.

If being open means that you have to purge your life of people, places, and/or things that no longer serve you, then do so. It takes courage to change, to recognize when your environment and influences have passed their expiration date and you need to let them go, so you can take a chance on life. Your future life. For your future self and those around you who matter most.

Everything coming into your life—good or bad—is tied, in some way, to what you believe you deserve. That can be a tough truth to accept. And to be clear, I'm not talking about life's tragedies; I'm talking about the everyday realities we create for ourselves. Sometimes it can be that you're too busy with the wrong environment. Or you allow influences from family, coworkers, or friends that are negative *to think for you* if you are being influenced to believe that there is simply no way for you to receive more, that "you'll never get married," that "you can't start that business," that "you can't be a 'good' working mom and simultaneously raise kids," that "you're not good enough," then that is exactly what will happen.

I challenge you to think about the things you want and bring your heart and mind into alignment with it. Doing so opens the floodgates of opportunities and abundance for you and when.

Of course, as we discussed in previous chapters there may be challenges that will make themselves known. It may not always be perfect. And that's okay. But the good news is ... you will succeed every single time when you face challenges with the attitude *"I can handle what comes my way."* You have to make a decision and commit to that. You can't keep that "open to possibilities" door cracked open, one foot in, one foot out, and expect that it will work.

You have to keep it open because you deserve everything you want in life, and there is nobody else in your life who can get it for you. Go ALL IN!

Your Right to Be Happy

We talked about the beauty of falling in love with yourself. We talked about leaving fear behind and eliminating barriers in your life in earlier chapters. In reality, every single thing in this life worth doing does require effort and the investment of your time. You have to be frank with yourself and take a hard look at who you are and what you are willing to do to accomplish your goals. Nothing is more important than getting your life together. At some point you're going to have to realize this if you haven't already.

Forget about other people and what they are saying is possible or impossible. Look at your own self and be honest—are you up for this? Are you going to pledge to your deserving self that you are going to do everything in your power to shed what restrains you and negatively affects you?

Are you going to wake up tomorrow morning and be grateful for the air in your lungs and show gratitude with kindness and love? Are you going to let your mind build your dreams into reality through visualization and meditation? Are you going to be thankful for the power of self-love? Are you going to go after the life you have always imagined but you were too scared to go after? Are you ready to do this?

When you are, you will feel the moment you open to receive what your heart desires. You will feel it almost as a physical sensation, and it will feel overwhelming. It might make you cry, it might make you laugh, you may become excited and overjoyed because you will feel with your body and mind the moment of realization that you are beautiful inside and out, that you are deserving, that you are loving and lovable, and that you have the right to be happy, just as God made you to be.

Time and again throughout this book I have talked about the power of prayer and trust in Our Creator. I prayed that God would use me and give me the words that I'm supposed to share in this book. No holding back.

God has carried me through everything. With that being said, I have often challenged my friends, family, and complete strangers who are open to discussing the conventional prayer that recites, *"God, I am not worthy of your love, just say the word and my soul shall be healed"* I struggle with this one. I chose not to recite 'I am not worthy,' because language shapes our reality. God's Word teaches us that we are loved, precious, and capable. I've spoken with pastors, priests, and other religious leaders about this, and while many found my perspective intriguing, no one could argue with the point I raise.

I understand why the prayer exists. It is an invitation to center us with humility. For we are all sinners. Consequently, your subconscious mind doesn't know what you *mean*—it only registers the words you say. So even if you know deep down that you are worthy, reciting the *opposite* sends mixed signals. This is why the language we use—both in prayer and in everyday life—matters! I love the Bible; I respect it deeply. I honor its teachings. To be clear, the point I am simply making is that language impacts us. This includes the underlying intention. For that reason, I choose a reframe that both preserves humility and affirms worth:

"Lord, I humbly welcome You into my life. Just say the word, and my soul will be healed."

Do you see the difference? I recognize that the Bible was written hundreds of years ago, and my intention is not to change it. (And no, I am not implying to change scripture. I can proudly say I am not worthy to do such a thing!) My growth in understanding the Scriptures has led me to embrace the power of language in prayer. For this reason, I continue to honor and include scriptures throughout this book.

I also firmly believe that the more blessings, opportunities, and abundance you want to attract, the more intentional you need to be with the words you speak and the thoughts you *choose* to entertain.

> **1 Peter 2:9 (NIV)** "But you are a chosen people, a royal priesthood, a holy nation, God's special possession, that you may declare the praises of him who called you out of darkness into his wonderful light." You are chosen. You are set apart. You are God's special possession—worthy of light, not shame.

God did not intend for us to carry guilt throughout our life, like chains that hold us back. God wants us to love and feel loved and confident in our pursuit. And when you are completely vulnerable with yourself and in front of God, when you show your true self, are unapologetically honest, when you see your naked soul through the prism of God's love, you will see yourself deserving and having the right to be happy.

The generational (and even culturally for some) guilt some of us carry that's often an exaggerated show of love to God by wallowing in our sins and mistakes, unable to forgive ourselves, is not bringing us closer to Him, nor closer to our own happiness. It drags us down instead, making us paralyzed in uncertainty and by our past mistakes. It prevents us from learning the lessons that will elevate us.

So you've made mistakes; so you have a past; now you have baggage. Yeah ... and SO WHAT?

We are all human. We all make mistakes. That's how you learn. That's how you grow. That is how you appreciate. That is why you, me, and everyone else have the free will to make bad choices and good choices. Being stuck with the bad choices you make will not move you forward. Making a different choice, there is where your power lies. God gave you free will.

You are so worthy. You are so deserving. You are so lovable. Just see yourself and bask in the glory of God's best creation—you.

So, what if you don't know what happiness is supposed to look like because you have not yet experienced it in your life. That doesn't mean that you can't move beyond your past trauma and build a better future. That is why you read this book. And I truly hope and believe with all my heart that you will see what I know is inside you, unleash it, build on it, and become the magnificent person you are meant to be, the person who, in turn, will inspire people around you.

Give yourself the grace that God has already bestowed upon you. Allow yourself to be happy, to be open to living the life you truly deserve. Continue to see in your mind's eye where it is that you want to be, what it feels like, and build on that. You are perfect the way you are, and God wants you to be happy above all else. Trust Him. Let Him guide you, and let yourself be loved.

Remember, He wants you to knock on His door and say, "I want to be happy"! You have the right to do that. Everyone does. It all starts with you, with the life you have been given, with the opportunity to open your eyes every morning and start again with a clean slate. Regardless of your age, if you're in your 20s, your 40s, 60s, or even 80s like my mom! You can change, right now, it's never too late. You just have to see it and believe it—and seize it. You get one life to live. One. Live it to your absolute fullest.

Be grateful for the little things, the privilege to wake up, to start your day and do better, be better, the opportunity to wake up and go again, one many are not so lucky to have. The big things, they will come. Find the joy and happiness in the little things that will make all the difference in the world in your relationship with yourself and everything around you. Just like when we get swept up at the beginning of a whirlwind romance, open your eyes and let the gratitude of everything around you wash over you.

Stop and look up. Truly see the beautiful sky above you. See the shapely dark clouds that are floating around as the heralds of life and relief by providing much-needed rain for the parched Earth underneath them. Take a moment to truly feel the warmth of the cup in your hand. The smiles at your kitchen table. Pay attention. Feel. Embrace the good and the bad because they both serve a purpose, and it is up to you to use that and build the life you have always wanted by allowing yourself to have the courage to be who you are.

Be happy today because today is the day. Today is when you make that new choice, you take that new step, and you start that new beginning.

- Be happy today because you are privileged to open your eyes in the morning.
- Be happy because you are given the gift of another day.

Tomorrow is not promised to anyone, but today is yours, and you better make it count.

Never Settle

Telling yourself that you have not settled when you so obviously have is one of the biggest lies you can tell yourself. Many have had rough childhoods. I got robbed of my childhood, too. But I outgrew and shed the difficult circumstances around me. I fought hard for a better life for my kids.

It's not because I'm super special, gifted, or even incredibly lucky (which, by the way, I do consider myself). It's because not for a single minute during my rough period did I let myself settle.

I did not know what was out there; nor did I know what tomorrow would bring. I did not know what my potential and limits were, but I knew darn straight that this could not be it. I knew that this situation was suffocating me, holding me back, hurting me. But this could not have been all there was for me. I was never going to allow that to be the end of it. And I didn't stop until I found out what I am capable of and how amazing my life could be.

I want the same for you. That is why I wrote this book. For the person who knows this cannot be it and they are searching for more. For the person who will do anything for their current life not to be the only life they could have.

I know very well the feeling of hunger from my childhood: The moment when all my savings as a child went to paying the electric bill so we wouldn't stay in the dark. I know the feeling of holding your breath for the other shoe to drop in an environment where uncertainty was the norm. And I knew, from the deepest regions of my soul, that I would try my absolute best to find what that "more" in my life could look like.

"There has to be more to life than this!"

This is the phrase that literally saved my life. It was also the start of making the mindset shift to get out of the circumstances I was in and to not settle with whatever cards I was dealt. It was my responsibility to do that—nobody else's.

Just like now, it is your responsibility to take the step, not settle.

It doesn't matter how much money you have or how famous you are. You can be unhappy, unsatisfied, lonely, and downright miserable. Money doesn't make you happy. Finding your purpose and going after it does.

The moment you settle is the moment you stop loving yourself. You certainly aren't loving anyone around you, no matter how much you are trying to convince yourself that you are doing this for someone else. How can you love anyone else if you aren't loving yourself? You are literally telling the universe that you deserve less. It doesn't matter what your circumstances are.

It doesn't matter how deserving you SAY you are. Your actions speak louder than words. If you are showing the universe and God that you are settling with where you are and who you are, this is what you will always get.

That is why I started my journey. You and I, we all have one life on this planet, with this environment, with the people we love now. You have this one chance now to make a true difference with where you are headed. Just think about your future 95-year-old self.

Ask that person, did you settle? See what your future self says. Did you take the risks worth taking, those risks that light your heart afire and skip a beat, the ones that make you smile just by the thought that you did it. Did you take them?

Are you now living life intentionally? Are you living your life with meaning? Are you living life on your terms? You know that you don't have to wait for anything or anyone to do so. You can start today, have the courage to live on your own terms, and find your true purpose. Raise the bar. Raise your standards for yourself and everyone in your life. Because until you do this, nothing will change, no matter how bad you want it. Do you want change? You have to change first. And I am not talking about changing your personality, but changing your choices, your decisions, and your actions.

Settling is something that starts with you. You hold the key to the "Yes or No," to the next step on a dead-end journey or the first step to your better self, better life, to your unconditional happiness.

If you take one thing from this book, never, ever settle for anything less than what your heart desires.

Celebrate Daily

I talked about so many things in this book. I talked about my own personal journey, how I discovered what more *there is to life, how I built the courage to go for it, and how I am helping others* reach their full potential too. We unpacked feelings, unresolved and resolved; we talked about approaches to hard things in life; we talked about approaches to easy things in life.

We talked about boundaries, happiness, and love. We talked about God and healing, gratitude, and forgiveness. We talked about the power of your subconscious mind to make a different choice, to "change the channel" in your journey to greatness so that you can have more of what you want.

So, what do you do with all this?

You show up and do it. And when you do it, you celebrate.

In our day and age, people don't celebrate small victories. Something grand has to happen … a graduation, a marriage, a birthday, a promotion. What about celebrating the small things?

- ✓ Hey, I woke up today feeling energized.
- ✓ Hey, I made the first step to learn how to open my new business.
- ✓ Hey, I mustered the courage to stand up for myself and set my boundaries today.
- ✓ Hey, I spoke up in a meeting and felt that my opinion mattered.
- ✓ Hey, I made that deal today.
- ✓ Hey, I set aside time to do my intentions in the morning.
- ✓ Hey, I made some progress this week.

Celebrate!!!

Underestimating the power of celebrating the small steps to the big goal is a mistake. You have to invest in yourself; it is one of the biggest gifts you can give yourself. The biggest return on investment you will ever make. And it does not have to cost you anything. You are lucky. Many people do not push themselves out of their comfort zone, but you did. You have to cheer yourself on every step of the way, not just the hard ones. Every step of the way is important.

These small pebbles build the giant road to success. Imagine you, building you. Like a home, where you build the foundation brick by brick, using bricks of immense quality, strong enough to weather any storm. That is what this book will do: Allow you to build and keep building a stronger, more powerful you.

Heck, celebrate the fact that you are here right now, reading this book and taking a chance on yourself in your journey. Celebrate that you have the courage to look for something beyond. Celebrate that you don't want to settle and you are reaching for more. Celebrate the crack in the door of you being open to receive that more. Because when you do that, one day soon, that door will be wide open, and everything will be possible.

It all starts with you and how proud you are of yourself. It's not just about the first and the last steps, as we are often told. All the steps in between are important; they are vital for your success. Because you have to muster the same strength to go on every time you take that next step forward; every time you are not just standing still but pushing for what you want. And that, my dear friend, is worth a celebration.

You want to know the best part of celebrating your victories? Momentum. And when you gain momentum, everything will start happening easier, faster, and better for you. This is when your whole being exudes that infectious energy that will move mountains for you. It's the kind of creative and exciting energy that you need flowing to accomplish the impossible.

That is why you have to cultivate it, to cherish it, to protect and grow it. That is how you stir the pot of the universe.

The magic, it's in you.

You can attend a million talks, seminars, and trainings; you can read hundreds of books; and you can attach thousands of inspirational quotes on your fridge and post them all over your social media, but if you don't do the work, if you don't invest yourself, in your own success, if you don't celebrate when it's hard and you make the tiniest progress forward, you won't be able to make it. And you CAN make it. You WILL make it. I know it. You know it. You just have to go for it.

- ✓ You can have it all, whatever all means to you.
- ✓ You can have the right balance and fulfillment in your life.
- ✓ You can live life on your own terms.

It might take some time. It will take some effort, but you can do it. And you should take the time to reflect on every single step that moves you forward, every single step that brings you closer to the life you were meant to have. Have courageous goals worth pursuing and remember although having goals is great and vital, it's not what will get you there, your commitment is what will ultimately get you there. Remember this. How committed you are is how likely you are to attain it. Stick with it; celebrating your journey in every moment, not just the good ones.

Celebrating your wins is like a coin in your motivation tank too. There are so many benefits to celebrating your wins. As you gain momentum because the universe is giving you more of what you are feeling, it will boost your confidence to do even more.

Dopamine levels increase when you celebrate your wins. Oxytocin and endorphins, too, are released into the bloodstream.

These, when combined, give you that euphoric feeling—this is your feel-good state. So celebrate your wins!

Water Your Garden

Living your life to the fullest and being open to more require effort—effort that can be fun. Think about your life as a garden. You plant your seeds with intention. You pull out the weeds that do not serve you. You water your garden to nourish it. Then, you enjoy the fruits of your labor. It really is *that* simple.

So how can one implement this in daily life?

- **Reflect**

    When you reflect in silence, the universe speaks to you the most. It can even be in the form of meditation. This is what sparks clarity.

    1. Look at your week and think about what went well. What are the highlights of your week?
    2. Now look at what roadblocks you had to overcome or will have to overcome. What challenges did you have, and how can you overcome them? What else can be possible?
    3. Be mindful of the questions you ask. Ask a great question, and you will get a great answer. Ask a lousy question, and well, I think you know what follows.

- **Show gratitude**

    Think about what went well this week and what you can be grateful for. Even if you had an awful week, I know you can find something that went well. Even the fact that you are here still breathing and have a chance to go again next week and do it differently. Feel gratitude for that simple fact.

This is one of the most important things you can do to celebrate daily. Whether you take the time to write your gratitude in your journal or share it with a friend in conversation, say it to yourself in the quiet of your mind, or share it with God in the privacy of your prayer, just do it. Show gratitude for the things you have and for those you don't because everything in your life is falling into place the way that it is meant to be. Find gratitude even in the storm and all that it is teaching you, and you will weather it that much easier, I promise.

- **Reward yourself**

    Rewarding yourself triggers positive emotions in your brain, underscoring the importance of celebrating your wins—big and small. So now you have a motivated reason to give yourself that gift.

    Go out to dinner with a friend or partner. Take a break and go on that extended lunch. Open that nice bottle of wine or drink your favorite mocktail. Go for a walk, or heck, go dancing. Even if it's in your kitchen!

- **Look ahead**

    Remember to always look forward, never look back. When you are driving, you cannot go where you are headed by looking in the rearview mirror, right?

    The important thing is to be better than who you were yesterday, to do better than you did before, to make better choices, and to change the channel for today, tomorrow, and the day after. What happened before, in the past, is beyond your control in the now. Yes, it is important to reflect on what you did that worked or didn't work. Data is valuable but it is not okay to dwell and stay in the past. Forget about what you did or did not do before. You have here and NOW. Focus on what you can improve and remember to access your remote to "change the channel" in every situation.

- **You choose how big you want to dream. Never restrain yourself, your capabilities, or your limits; likewise, never let anyone do the same, either.**

    What you dream of is within your reach, and you should never hide behind the mask of the "can't" and "won't." That "dream" is your desire. Desire is the first step in achieving anything you want. You can, and you will achieve everything you wish to when you let yourself believe that you can. It's not about magic, it's about science, and I proved to you time and again that what you put out there is what you will get back. Be careful what channel your consciousness is tuned to. If you don't like it ... change it! It is up to you whether to stay in a negative circumstance or do whatever it takes to get out of it. Be relentless, plant your seeds. You will see them flourish, because you chose to change it. *It starts with you.*

- **Believe**

    No amount of pep-talk and inspiration can help you get the life you want for yourself if you don't believe that you can. You have to believe in yourself; you have to believe that what you want is possible. You have to train your subconscious mind to help you on this journey. Work with it, not against it. Open your heart, your mind, and your soul. Be intentional about what you feed your mind. Give it a go.

If you feed it with negativity and denial, instead of *positivity and drive*, if you don't focus on your grit and work with your grace, you won't achieve your goals. Period. But if you do work with the amazing gift that Our Creator has given to you—your mind—you will achieve amazing things. You have to trust in Our Creator, no matter who God is for you. God has your back and loves you. Believing in a higher power will bring you so much more.

I know that many great things lie ahead for you. And, yes, even challenges but I also know that *you got this*! I am rooting for you, big time. Most importantly, I know God is rooting for you too.

I know that you will make things happen with your life that nobody ever dreamed and imagined you could, simply because you learned about the power that lies within you for *More*. Your potential is greater than any challenge you could ever face. Your faith, focus, and action will unlock opportunities you haven't even imagined. Believe in yourself, because God already believes in you and the best is yet to come.

Now go out there and be great!
I cannot wait to see what you do with your life.
Join the movement! Tag me on social!

Make things happen!

...Success is something you attract
by the person you become.
Success is not something you pursue.
It's like chasing a butterfly.
You can't quite catch it.
Success is something you attract
- by becoming an attractive person.
     Motivational speaker, the late Jim Rohn

"*Do not conform to the pattern of this world, but be transformed by the renewing of your mind. Then you will be able to test and approve what God's will is—his good, pleasing and perfect will.*"

     —*Romans 12:2*

Acknowledgments

This book has been the most rewarding endeavor I have ever embarked on. I didn't walk it alone. To my husband, thank you for your unconditional love and for supporting me with my craziest, most audacious dreams. For my four kids, you show me the meaning of unconditional love. You are my biggest fans, and your support means the world. Thank you for inspiring me to be my best version. This book carries your fingerprints.

To my mom, who taught me faith, resilience, and the power of love, I am eternally grateful and thank God for you every day.

To those who stood beside me with encouragement, honesty, and love—whether a sibling, friend, mentor, or supporter—your presence in the unseen moments has meant more than words can say.

To my readers holding this book. This book is my heart laid bare for you. These pages hold pieces of my story, my struggle, and my soul. If even one line or sentence wakes something up inside you, reminds you of who you are, or what you're capable of, then every tear, every rewrite, every sleepless night, and every vulnerable word was worth it. This is for the version of you who almost gave up. My hope is that these words meet you where you are and help you rise, reminding you of your strength, your voice, and the purpose that's always been within you.

And to God—this was always Yours. You called me to this, gave me the courage to write this and the grace to finish it. Every page is a testimony of Your faithfulness.

With love and deep gratitude,
Diana Pagano

About the Author

Known for empowering people to make bold moves and crush barriers, action-driven mindset coach, author, keynote speaker, and the host of the *MAKE THINGS HAPPEN* podcast, Diana Pagano, is a force for transformation.

As the founder of the *MAKE THINGS HAPPEN*™ movement, Diana equips individuals and organizations with the necessary strategies to break free from limiting beliefs and step into empowering mindsets. Diana challenges people to stop settling and start living the life they were destined for. Her actionable tools for unlocking next-level performance and unstoppable energy are backed by the latest brain research and proven neuroscience strategies.

A proud first-generation Mexican-American from San Diego, Diana grew up navigating instability as her parents constantly faced financial struggles. She moved thirteen times by the age of seventeen. Refusing to be a victim of circumstances, Diana converted adversity into fuel that propelled her towards a life of achievement.

A once single mom, Diana broke records during rookie real estate agent years, by increasing her income 10X in just *twelve* months! She then went on to apply her proven strategies for life and business success to help scale a multimillion-dollar language company by 5×, as Executive Vice President. Now she uses that same fire, and a lifetime of knowledge to help others rise to their potential to achieve extraordinary measurable results. Her journey is the driving force behind her mission. It's also a testament to what's possible with vision, discipline, resilience, and relentless purpose.

Today, Diana inspires audiences around the world through her *MAKE THINGS HAPPEN* podcast, workshops, and keynote talks. Whether speaking on stage, leading workshops, or guiding teams, Diana doesn't just motivate—she activates, igniting breakthrough moments that move people - from hesitation to bold, immediate action and next level performance.

Diana lives in Connecticut with her husband and their two children, and is also a proud mother to her two oldest children in their 20s. Anchored in her faith, she leads with heart, lives with purpose, and continues to empower others to make things happen—one breakthrough at a time.

Learn more at DianaPagano.com.

Index

A

abundance, 217
abusive marriage, 2
abusive relationship, 116
achieved success, xvii, 60, 62–63
adrenaline, 1, 134
Angelou, Maya, 58
anger, 52, 81, 118, 140
anxiety, 138
   attacks, 51, 133
   breath, 133–135
   cause, 135
   combat, 138
   disorganized or procrastinate, 137
   exercise, 139–140
   feelings of, 132, 133, 135
   overstressing and maintaining, 136
   proactive and productive way, 136
   unmet obligations, 137
apologize, 48, 54, 93, 97, 98, 101, 109, 175, 206
attitudes, 11, 14–17, 70, 78, 84, 89, 90, 103, 115, 117, 154, 214
attracts, 10–16
authentic
   genuine and, 205
   happiness, 205
   self, 205, 208
   value, 207
automatic negative thoughts (ANTs), 76
   awareness, 137, 174
   conscious, 177
   mind-body, 145
   neural network, 177
   power, 137

B

Bandler, Richard, Dr., 119
barriers
   breaking the chains of guilt, 190–192
   dreams, 188
   fear, 194–198
   fortify boundaries, 193
   guilt-free living, 193–194
   neural pathways, 186
   overcome, 190
   perceived, 189
   real-life, 186
   self-imposed, 186, 188
beliefs, 4–6, 231
   change, xii
   false, 6–10, 15, 22,
   limiting, 10, 44, 121, 231
   control, 11
   barriers, 188
   blessings, 217
   good or bad, 214
   living your life, 227
   meditation, 145
   opportunities, 217
   in yourself, 227
Bible, 149, 150, 216
blessings, 138, 154, 161, 217
brain's "alarm center," 135
bravery, 125–130
breaking point, 17
breathing techniques, 138
Bruce Almighty (Carey), 159
business meeting, 62

C

career choices, 36
caregivers, xvii
Carey, Jim, 159
Carroll, Lewis, 21
Catholic faith, 149
celebrate
    gratitude, 226
    momentum, 223
    power of, 223
    for small things, 222
    victories, 222, 223
    wins, 224–226
change the channel, xvi, xviii, 14, 20, 70, 77, 111–130, 155, 174, 195, 196, 198, 209, 222, 226
changing catalyst, 24–28
childhood beliefs, 15, 19
childhood experience, 8–10
childhood trauma, 9
Chin, F., 160
Chou, R., 160
chronic migraines, 135
client meetings, 158
client relationships, 48, 158
Coderre, Terrence, 75
collateral damage, 47
combat anxiety, 138
commitments, 17, 50, 61, 138, 139, 193, 207, 215, 224
confidence, 4, 5, 18, 20, 35, 59–64, 74, 81, 84, 86, 90, 115
conscious awareness, 177
conventional prayer, 216
conviction, 56, 120, 153, 158, 159
customer meeting, 171

D

decision making
    single mom, 22
    success or growth, 94
depression, 135, 170, 200
Diamond, Marie, ix, x
    dreams, xi, xii, xiii, xiv, xv, 5, 29, 36, 58–60, 68, 69, 73, 83, 90–101, 103–109, 130, 132, 141, 153, 157, 179, 180, 182, 188, 189, 194, 196, 204, 208–210, 212, 215, 227–229
Dweck, Carol, 76
Dyer, Wayne, Dr., 73

E

ego, 7
Einstein, Albert, 129
emotional baggage, 191
emotions
    conscious thoughts, 177
    feelings and, 13, 71
    positive, 226
    state, 82, 116
empower yourself, 154
energy, 11–13, 63
    and frequency, 70
    internal, 86
    shifts, 63
    vibrational, 13–15, 32, 63, 80, 83, 156
enteric brain, 140
enthusiasm, 1
euphoric feeling, 225
exercise
    anxiety and stress, 139
    breathing, 146
    gratitude, 203
    lifestyle, 138–139
exhaustion, 2, 46, 108
experiences
    childhood, 8–10
    emotions, 31, 76
    failure, 4, 6, 72
    feeling, 65, 78
    God's presence, 151
    guilt, 191
    sadness, 4, 6, 12
    sharing, 4, 16
    spiritual, 163
    transformational, 211
    traumatic, 75

F

failure/success, 6
    word, 123–125
faith, 190, 203
    Catholic, 149
    in God, 151, 154, 190, 203
fake fear, 32
false beliefs, 6–10, 15, 22
False Evidence Appearing Real (F.E.A.R.), 132, 133, 195, 197
    family business, 104, 105
    family dynamics, 143
    family vacation, 17, 143, 201

Index

fear
  childhood trauma and, 9
  or doubt, 59, 71
  of failure, 9, 33, 107
  fake, 32
  fearful thoughts, 194
  feeling of, 198
  gratitude and, 196
  vs hope, 127
  and hopelessness, 52
  negative thoughts, 13, 31
  peace, 196
  symptoms of, 194
  uncertainty and, 197
  fearful thought, 13, 31, 80, 194
  feel anxious, 133, 135
feelings
  of confidence, 63
  control, 51
  of depression and anxiety, 76
  and emotions, 13, 71
  euphoric, 225
  of fear, 198
  fearful to anger, 52
  of freedom, 18
  of gratitude, 70, 202
  gut, 17
  of happiness, 69
  of hope, 119
  of hunger, 220
  of inadequacy, 53, 73
  of lack/fear, 118
  prayer, 160, 161
feel overwhelming, 215
fight-or-flight response, 134
financial stress, 98
fortify boundaries, 193
frustrated, 14, 76, 81, 82, 108, 163, 183, 195, 201

G
Gabana, N.T., 200
Garbage In, Garbage Out (GIGO), 128
generational guilt, 217
goals, 91
  goal achievement, 7, 20, 31, 38, 40, 41, 52, 86, 99, 104, 129, 148, 183, 227
  goal setting, 41
God, 149, 150–155, 161
  God potential, 152–155
  God's best creation, 218
  God's love, 217
  God's Word, 216
grateful, 225
gratitude, 14, 62, 69–71, 138, 142–143, 166, 171
  celebrate daily, 226
living your life, 225–226
"Gratitude Grapes," 202
grit exercise, 40, 41, 122, 124, 174, 227
guilt, 1, 2, 47, 48, 92, 93, 118, 144, 190–194, 217
  breaking the chains of, 190–192
  free living, 193–194
  generational, 217
gut brain connection, 140
gut feeling, 17

H
happiness, 65–66, 218
  authentic, 205
  check in yourself, 81–87
  deserving of, 206
  exercise, 78–81
  experience sadness, 6
  focusing on, 67–75
  in little things, 219
  negative thoughts, 75–78
  not suffering, 26
  peace and, 33
  unconditional, 221
hardship, 18, 22, 51, 57, 105
healing, 150
  during difficult times, 150
  gratitude and forgiveness, 222
healthy gut, 140
heartbreak, 18, 64
Hill, Napoleon, 172
Holy Spirit, 149
holy trinity of good living, 140
hormone, stress, 61, 134
human experience, 16, 31, 53, 54, 65, 76, 124, 191

I
imperfections, 16, 35, 54, 85, 86, 98, 137, 152, 205, 206
impossible, xiv, 7, 27, 44, 45, 71, 81, 89–91, 94, 106, 113, 136, 186–189, 196, 211, 215, 224
information sharing, 58
inspiration, 147–148

internal energy, 86
interpersonal growth, 82

J
job description, 132
job juggling, 192
Joel Wong, Y., 200
Johnson, Dwayne "The Rock," 100, 101, 107
journal, 142–143
journey, 4, 10, 15, 17, 25, 28–38, 40, 49, 55, 64, 72, 73, 86, 91, 92, 96, 98, 104, 106, 107, 113
Judaism, 149

K
"Keep It Simple and Succulent" (k.i.s.a.s.), 102
kind, 10, 102
King, Stephen, 58
knowledge, 6, 10, 11, 44, 98, 104, 113, 129

L
lack of imagination, 58
language, power of, 217
Lao Tzu, 29
lies, 6–10, 73, 76, 97, 219
life-changing choices, 22
life experiences, 8, 44, 54
life-threatening situations, 48, 119, 134
life worth living
    authentic, 204–208
    cultures, 210
    grateful, 201–204
    gratitude, 200–201
    heart desires, 209
    life partner, 209
mediocre, 199, 209
living your life
look forward, 226
loving yourself, 10, 192, 213, 221

M
mediocre life, 199, 209
meditation, 225
memory, 5, 22, 23, 25, 70, 75, 76, 97, 196
mental activity, of visualization, 30
mental attitude, 117
mental control, 134
mental detox, 1421 143
mental health, 87, 129, 140, 142, 200, 202

mental regulation, 138
mental rehearsal phase, 171, 172
mental state, 80, 119, 144
metamorphosis, 58
micro-biome impact, 141
mind-body awareness, 145
mindfulness, 145
mind positive thoughts, 141
mindset
    mindset shifts, xiv, 220
    resilient mindset, 76, 175
mommy guilt, 192
Mother Teresa, 76, 129

N
negative beliefs, 7, 30
negative emotions, 12, 13, 75, 76, 81
negative expectations, 10
negative feelings, 163
negative language, 122
negative relationship, 97
negative self-talk, 30, 31
negative thinking, 90, 194
negative thoughts, 13, 30–32, 44, 70, 75–81, 109, 122, 126, 127, 135, 140, 174
neural pathways, 186
neuro-cognitive changes, 160
neurological response, 172
neuroplasticity, 13
neuroscience, 13, 53, 231
neurotransmitter, 141
nurturing, 23, 48, 69, 115, 142

O
obstacles. see barriers
Our Creator, 57, 95, 98, 125, 150, 154, 157, 159–161, 163, 164, 216, 227
overstressed, 108, 136
over-thinking, 108
Owen, J., 200

P
Pagano, Diana, ix, x, xviii, 230, 231
pain
    avoid, 53
    builds resilience, 50
    memory traces of, 75, 76
    physical or mental, 161
    of rejection, 32
    shared, 56

Index

and suffering, 54
tolerance, 160
transition, 112
is your power, xv
parasympathetic system, 135
Paulus, Trina, 58
peace, xii, 3, 23, 32, 33, 49, 55, 67, 87, 128, 131, 142, 144–148, 159, 165, 192, 194–196
perceived barriers, 189
perception, 10, 13, 32, 116, 138, 189
perfection, 3, 14, 102
personal conflict, 23
personal growth, xvii, 10, 55, 73, 79, 82, 84
personal relationships, 55
personal success, 86, 102
positive beliefs, 7
positive feeling, 14
positive mindset, 81
positive self-talk, 31, 61
positive thinking, ix, 53, 90, 164, 184
positive thoughts, xvii, 13, 35, 70, 77, 127, 136
positivity and drive, 227
power
  awareness, 131
  of celebrate, 223
  of conviction, 56
  of personal values, 96
  of prayer, 156. 158, 159–163, 216, 217
  of visualization, 169, 170, 179–184
  of words, 117–123
prayer, 156, 158
  power of, 159–163
  power of language in, 217
  purposeful, 164
professional relationships, 82
psychological trauma, 51
Purkey, William W., 75

Q
questions, reflect on, 39–40

R
RAS. See Reticular Activating System (RAS)
real estate
  business, 102, 121, 157
  career, xiv, 2, 36, 103, 158
  real estate agent, 2, 232
real-life barriers, 186

receive
  good or bad, 214
recovery, xviii, 119, 184
regret factor, 99–100
relationships
  abusive, 25, 116
  business or personal, 47
  client, 48, 158
  loving and respectful, 31
  negative, 97
  personal, 55
  professional, 82
  psychologically, 9
relaxation, meditation, 146–147
resilience, 40, 50, 55, 57, 62, 94, 105, 114, 119, 124, 152–154, 229, 232
respect, 48, 53, 120, 216
Reticular Activating System (RAS), 123, 176–178, 209
retrocausality, 40
Rihanna, 84
road map, building, 38–41, 74
Rohn, Jim, 228

S
sadness experience, 4, 6, 12
scriptures, 150, 155–157, 163–167, 217
self-acceptance, 86
self-affirmation, 63
self-awareness, xvii, 86
self-care, 46, 82, 85
self-compassion, 55, 81, 102
self-confidence, 84
self-criticism, 68, 191
self-discipline, 61, 165
self-discovery, 10, 11, 92, 97, 157
self-doubt, 15, 18, 32, 36, 128
self-empathy, 102
self-esteem, 60, 84
self-forgiveness, 191
self-image, 5, 7, 86
self-imposed barriers, 186, 188, 190
self-inspecting microscope, 102
self-love, 55, 85, 87, 91, 154, 178, 215
self-prioritizing, 47
self-reflection, 11, 60, 86, 179, 191
self-sabotage, 76–78, 127, 161, 198
self-talk, 51, 108, 156, 157, 190
  monitor your, 61–62
  negative, 30, 31
  positive, 31, 61

self-worth, 10, 63, 68
shifts, mindset, xiv, 220
Silverstein, Shel, 89
single mom, 207
Sirleaf, Ellen Johnson, 59
social media, 7, 53, 73, 85, 136, 142, 177, 224
sorrow, 18
sparking anxiety, 132
spiritual connection practice, 164
spirituality, 150
spiritual practice, 145, 160, 164
stress, 2, 12, 49, 61, 81, 98, 108, 115, 117, 132, 136, 137, 139, 141, 147, 170, 176, 192
stress hormone, 134
subconscious mind, 172, 175, 216, 222, 227
success
    personal, 86, 102
successful person, 111, 129

T

teaching knowledge, 10
Tesla, Nicola, 11
Think and Grow Rich (Hill), 172
thoughts
    change thoughts, 129
    control, 20
    replacing, 80
tough love, 8
transformational shift, xii
traumatic experiences, 75
trouble sleeping, 135

U

unconditional love, 142, 208
uncontrolled fear, 31
Universal Beginning, 160
unmet obligations, 137
unquestioned belief, 38

V

vacations, 9, 17, 96, 136, 143, 148, 178, 201
vibrational energy, 13–15, 32, 63, 80, 83, 156
victim mentality, 57
vision board, 103, 104, 211
visual deception, 53
visualization, 170, 180
    brain, 175
    golf, 174–175
    intensity, 171
    mental activity of, 30
    mind, 175, 176
    momentum's power source, 176–179
    outcome, 172
    power of, 169, 170, 179–184
Vujicic, Nick, 28

W

Walsch, Neale Donald, 59
Walt Disney, 58
Waqas, M., 160
well-being, 47, 62, 67, 68, 76, 77, 122, 131, 141, 160, 192, 193, 200, 202
willpower, 59, 61, 92
words
    of possibility, 118
    power of, 117–123
working hard, 97
working mother, 191

Y

your identity, 61, 66, 94, 115, 116, 163
yourself
    commit to, 50
    dreams, 91–98
    empower, 154
    kind to, 85
    loving, 10, 192, 213, 221
    taking care of, 45–50